Leadership:
The Power of
Emotional
Intelligence

Also by Daniel Goleman from More Than Sound

The Brain and Emotional Intelligence: New Insights

Better Parents, Better Spouses, Better People with Daniel Siegel

Knowing Our Emotions, Improving Our World with Paul Ekman

Training the Brain: Cultivating Emotional Intelligence with Richard Davidson

Good Work: Aligning Skills and Values with Howard Gardner

The Inner Compass for Ethics and Excellence with Naomi Wolf

Socially Intelligent Computing with Clay Shirky

Rethinking Education with George Lucas

Leading the Necessary Revolution with Peter Senge

Ecological Awareness: Dialogues on Ecological Intelligence

Of Interest:

Resonant Leadership: Inspiring Others Through Emotional Intelligence by Richard Boyatzis

Available at morethansound.net

Leadership:
The Power of Emotional Intelligence

SELECTED WRITINGS

BY

DANIEL GOLEMAN

Published by More Than Sound LLC

Northampton MA

www.morethansound.net

Images by Tracy Lee

Leadership: The Power of Emotional Intelligence

Selected Writings / Daniel Goleman

1st Edition

ISBN 978-1-934441-17-6

TABLE OF CONTENTS

(1) A Surprising Synergy

9

(2) Managing With Heart

16

(3) What Makes a Leader?

25

(4) Leadership That Gets Results

40

(5) The Group IQ

61

(6) Primal Leadership

67

(7) The Social Brain

82

(8) The Sweet Spot for Achievement

85

(9) Developing Emotional Intelligence

99

(Appendix) Leadership Competencies

102

— A SURPRISING SYNERGY —

I remember having the thought, just before *Emotional Intelligence* was published, that if one day I overheard a conversation in which two strangers used the words "emotional intelligence" and both understood what it meant, I would have succeeded in spreading the concept more widely into the culture. Little did I know.

The phrase emotional intelligence, or its casual shorthand EQ, has become ubiquitous, showing up in settings as unlikely as the cartoon strips Dilbert and Zippy the Pinhead, and in Roz Chast's sequential art in The New Yorker. I've seen boxes of toys that claim to boost a child's EQ; lovelorn personal ads sometimes trumpet it in those seeking prospective mates. I once found a quip about EQ printed on a shampoo bottle in my hotel room.

Perhaps the biggest surprise for me has been the impact of EI (the abbreviation I prefer) in the world of business. The Harvard Business Review has hailed emotional intelligence as "a ground-breaking, paradigm-shattering idea," and one of the most influential business ideas of the decade.

The decade after the 1995 publication of *Emotional Intelligence* saw a surge in applications of the concept to the workplace, particularly leadership screening, selection and development. And with this booming interest there grew a mini-industry of consultants and coaches, some selling their services by making claims that far outstripped the data. To set the story straight, I wrote a new introduction to the 10th anniversary edition of *Emotional Intelligence*. By that time there was an understandable backlash to the EI concept – and the exaggerated claims being made for it – among some academic psychologists. Only now, with a steady stream of better data, has much of the criticism ebbed, as a more empirical picture of the benefits of EI emerges from sound research.

The Rutgers University-based Consortium for Research on Emotional Intelligence in Organizations (CREIO) has led the way in catalyzing this scientific work, collaborating with organizations that range from the Office of Personnel Management in the Federal government to American Express.

When I wrote *Emotional Intelligence*, my main focus was new findings on the brain and emotions, particularly their implications for child development and schools. But I included a chapter on how this then-new concept informed our understanding of leadership, "Managing With Heart." The interest in the business community was so great that my next two books were on the implications of emotional intelligence for the workplace (*Working With Emotional Intelligence*) and on leadership itself (*Primal Leadership: Leading With Emotional Intelligence*). *Managing With Heart* – excerpted here in Chapter 2 – includes some practical advice on giving constructive feedback – and the consequences of giving critiques poorly. It offers a concrete example of the difference between leading with emotional intelligence, and without.

There are now three main models of EI, with dozens of variations. Each represents a different perspective. That of Peter Salovey and John Mayer rests firmly in the tradition of intelligence shaped by the original work on IQ a century ago. The model put forth by Reuven Bar-On grew from his research on well-being. And my own model focuses at the behavioral level, on performance at work and in organizational leadership, melding EI theory with decades of research on modeling the competencies that set star performers apart from average.

As I proposed in *Working with Emotional Intelligence*, EI abilities – rather than IQ or technical skills – emerge as the "discriminating" competency that best predicts who among a group of very smart people will lead most ably. If you scan the competencies that organizations around the world have independently determined identify their star leaders, you discover that indicators of IQ and technical skill drop toward the bottom of the list the higher the position. (IQ and technical expertise are much stronger predictors of excellence in lower-rung jobs.)

At the very highest levels, competence models for leadership typically consist of anywhere from 80 to 100 percent EI-based abilities. As the head of research at a global executive search firm put it, "CEOs are hired for their intellect and business expertise – and fired for a lack of emotional intelligence."

In *Working with Emotional Intelligence* I also proposed an expanded framework that reflects how the fundamentals of EI – that is, self-awareness, self-management, social awareness, and the ability to manage relationships – translate into on-the-job success. This framework is illustrated by the figure at the end of the chapter.

The business community's fascination with emotional intelligence, particularly for leaders, caught the attention of editors at the Harvard Business Review, who asked me to write more on the subject. My resulting 1998 Review article, *What Makes a Leader?*, has had surprising impact as well. It quickly became one of the most-requested reprints in the Review's history, and has been included in several leadership anthologies the Review has issued, including a collection of ten "must-read" articles from their pages. You'll find it in Chapter 3.

David McClelland, my mentor at Harvard, studied the motives that drove successful entrepreneurs – and was himself entrepreneurial, co-founding a research and consulting outfit called McBer, which applied the competence modeling method to the organizational world. That company later became part of the Hay Group, a global consulting firm, and the research arm of McBer has become the McClelland Institute, under the leadership of other former McClelland students Jim Burrus, Mary Fontaine, and Ruth Jacobs (now Malloy). As interest in the emotional intelligence competencies mushroomed, they shared with me data they had collected on business performance and leadership styles from thousands of executives, which I reported in the Harvard Business Review article, *Leadership That Gets Results* – reprinted here in Chapter 4.

In an economy driven by knowledge work, value gets created through the efforts of teams. This puts the focus on the "group IQ," a concept devised by Robert Sternberg and Wendy Williams at Yale. The group IQ represents the sum total of each team member's best talents contributed at full force. But what determines the actual productivity of that team is not its theoretical potential – that is, the group IQ – but rather how well that team coordinates its efforts. In other words, interpersonal harmony. I originally explored the dynamics of the group IQ in *Emotional Intelligence*, and then returned to the emotional dynamics of teams from the perspective of the styles of team leaders. You'll find these dynamics detailed in Chapter 5.

While *Emotional Intelligence* in large part reported on the findings of a then-new field, affective neuroscience, my 2003 book, *Social Intelligence*, was prompted by the emergence of exciting findings from another new field, social neuroscience. This branch of brain research began to look at how brains behave while we interact, and the result was a flood of new discoveries about the brain's social circuitry. Those findings had great implications in light of another set of discoveries about the relationship between the brain's centers for thought and for emotions, as you'll find in Chapter 8.

As I reported in *The Brain and Emotional Intelligence: New Insights*, the states of disengagement (epidemic in some workplaces), and of frazzle from too much stress (also epidemic) both disable the brain's prefrontal zones, the site of comprehension, focus, learning and creativity. On the other hand, as explained in Chapter 7, in the zone for flow the brain operates at peak cognitive efficiency, and people perform at their best.

This redefines the essential task of a leader: to help people get and stay in the brain zone where they can work at their best.

As you'll read in Chapter 6, I detailed this task in the book *Primal Leadership*, written with my colleagues Annie McKee and Richard Boyatzis. Effective leaders, we argued, create a resonance with those they lead, a neural harmony that facilitates flow.

Finally, there's the question of how a leader can develop further strengths in emotional intelligence. Here the good news from brain science is neuroplasticity: the insight that the brain continues to grow and shape itself throughout life. A systematic learning process, described here in Chapter 9, a selection from *The Brain and Emotional Intelligence*, can facilitate such leadership development at any point in a career – or life.

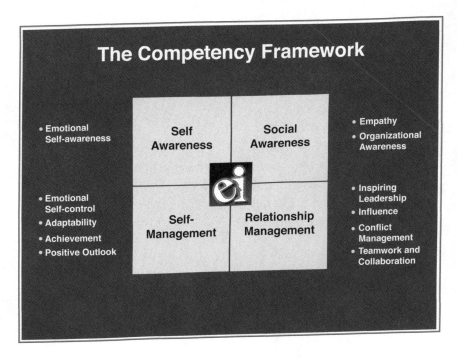

Most elements of every emotional intelligence model fit within these four generic domains: self-awareness, self-management, social awareness, and relationship management. Based on each of these core abilities are learned workplace competencies that distinguish the most successful leaders.

While our emotional intelligence determines our potential for learning the fundamentals of self-mastery and the like, our emotional competence shows how much of that potential we have mastered in ways that translate into on-the-job capabilities. To be adept at an emotional competence like customer service or teamwork requires an underlying ability in EI fundamentals, such as social awareness and relationship management. But emotional *competencies are learned abilities: simply having social awareness or skill at managing relationships does not guarantee that one has mastered the additional learning required to handle a customer adeptly or to resolve a conflict. One simply has the potential to become skilled at these competencies.*

So an underlying EI ability is necessary, though not sufficient, to manifest a given competency or job skill. A cognitive analog would be the student who has excellent spatial abilities yet never learns geometry, let alone becomes an architect. Likewise one can be highly empathic yet poor at, say, handling long-term client relationships.

For those ultra-dedicated souls wanting to understand how my current model nests the dozen or so key leadership emotional competencies within the four EI clusters, see the Appendix.

— MANAGING WITH HEART —

Adapted from Emotional Intelligence

Melburn McBroom was a domineering boss, with a temper that intimidated those who worked with him. That fact might have passed unremarked had McBroom worked in an office or factory. But McBroom was an airline pilot.

One day in 1978 McBroom's plane was approaching Portland, Oregon when he noticed a problem with the landing gear. So McBroom went into a holding pattern, circling the field at a high altitude while he fiddled with the mechanism.

As McBroom obsessed about the landing gear, the plane's fuel gauges steadily approached the empty level. But his copilots were so fearful of McBroom's wrath that they said nothing, even as disaster loomed. The plane crashed, killing ten people.

Today the story of that crash is told as a cautionary tale in the safety training of airline pilots.[2] In 80 percent of airline crashes, pilots make mistakes that could have been prevented, particularly if the crew worked together more harmoniously. Teamwork, open lines of communication, cooperation, listening, and speaking one's mind – rudiments of social intelligence – are now emphasized in training pilots, along with technical prowess.

The cockpit is a microcosm of any working organization. But lacking the dramatic reality check of an airplane crash, the destructive effects of miserable morale, intimidated workers, or arrogant bosses – or any of the dozens of other permutations of emotional deficiencies in the workplace – can go largely unnoticed by those outside the immediate scene. But the costs can be read in signs such as decreased productivity, an increase in missed deadlines, mistakes and mishaps, and an exodus of employees to more congenial settings. There is, inevitably, a cost to the bottom line from low levels of emotional intelligence on the job. When it is rampant, companies can crash and burn.

The cost-effectiveness of emotional intelligence is a relatively new idea for business, one some managers may find hard to accept. A study of 250 executives found that most felt their work demanded "their heads but not their hearts." Many said they feared that feeling empathy or compassion for those they worked with would put them in conflict with their organizational goals. One felt the idea of sensing the feelings of those who worked for him was absurd – it would, he said, "be impossible to deal with people." Others protested that if they were not emotionally aloof they would be unable to make the "hard" decisions that business requires – although the likelihood is that they would deliver those decisions more humanely.[3]

That study was done in the 1970s, when the business environment was very different. My argument is that such attitudes are outmoded, a luxury of a former day; a new competitive reality is putting emotional intelligence at a premium in the workplace and in the marketplace.

As Shoshona Zuboff, a psychologist at Harvard Business School, pointed out to me, "Corporations have gone through a radical revolution within this century, and with this has come a corresponding transformation of the emotional landscape. There was a long period of managerial domination of the corporate hierarchy when the manipulative, jungle-fighter boss was rewarded. But that rigid hierarchy started breaking down in the 1980s under the twin pressures of globalization and information technology. The jungle fighter symbolizes where the corporation has been; the virtuoso in interpersonal skills is the corporate future."

Some of the reasons are patently obvious – imagine the consequences for a working group when someone is unable to keep from exploding in anger or has no sensitivity about what the people around him are feeling. All the deleterious effects of agitation on thinking for an individual operate in the workplace too: When emotionally upset, people cannot remember, attend, learn, or make decisions clearly. As one management consultant put it, "Stress makes people stupid."

On the positive side, imagine the benefits for work of being skilled in the basic emotional competencies – being attuned to the feelings of those we deal with, being able to handle disagreements so they do not escalate, having the ability to get into flow states while doing our work. Leadership is not domination, but the art of persuading people to work toward a common goal. And, in terms of managing our own career, there may be nothing more essential than recognizing our deepest feelings about what we do – and what changes might make us more truly satisfied with our work.

THE ART OF THE CRITIQUE

He was a seasoned engineer, heading a software development project, presenting the result of months of work by his team to the company's vice president for product development. The men and women who had worked long days week after week were there with him, proud to present the fruit of their hard labor.

But as the engineer finished his presentation, the vice-president turned to him and asked sarcastically, "How long have you been out of graduate school? These specifications are ridiculous. They have no chance of getting past my desk."

The engineer, utterly embarrassed and deflated, sat glumly through the rest of the meeting, reduced to silence. The men and women on his team made a few desultory – and some hostile – remarks in defense of their effort. The vice president was then called away and the meeting broke up abruptly, leaving a residue of bitterness and anger.

For the next two weeks the engineer was obsessed by the vice president's remarks. Dispirited and depressed, he was convinced he would never get another assignment of importance at the company, and was thinking of leaving, even though he enjoyed his work there. Finally the engineer went to see the vice-president, reminding him of the meeting, his critical remarks, and their demoralizing effect. Then he made a carefully worded inquiry: "I'm a little confused by what you were trying to accomplish. I assume you were not just trying to embarrass me – did you have some other goal in mind?"

The vice president was astonished – he had no idea that his remark, which he meant as a throwaway line, had been so devastating. In fact, he thought the software plan was promising, but needed more work – he hadn't meant to dismiss it as utterly worthless at all. He simply had not realized, he said, how poorly he had put his reaction, nor that he had hurt anyone's feelings. And, belatedly, he apologized.[4]

It's a question of feedback, really, of people getting the information essential to keep their efforts on track. In its original sense in systems theory, feedback meant the exchange of data about how one part of a system is working, with the understanding that one part affects all others in the system, so that any part heading off course could be changed for the better. In a company everyone is part of the system, and so feedback is the lifeblood of the organization – the exchange of information that lets people know if the job they are doing is going well or needs to be fine-tuned, upgraded, or redirected entirely. Without feedback people are in the dark; they have no idea how they stand with their boss, with their peers, or in terms of what is expected of them, and any problems will only get worse as time passes.

In a sense, criticism is one of the most important tasks a manager has. Yet it's also one of the most dreaded and put off. And, like the sarcastic vice-president, too many managers have poorly mastered the crucial art of feedback. This deficiency has a great cost: just as the emotional health of a couple depends on how well they air their grievances, so do the effectiveness, satisfaction, and productivity of people at work depend on how they are told about nagging problems. Indeed, how criticisms are given and received goes a long way in determining how satisfied people are with their work, with those they work with, and with those to whom they are responsible.

THE WORST WAY TO MOTIVATE SOMEONE o———

The emotional vicissitudes at work in marriage also operate in the workplace, where they take similar forms. Criticisms are voiced as personal attacks rather than complaints that can be acted upon; there are ad hominem charges with dollops of disgust, sarcasm, and contempt; both give rise to defensiveness and dodging of responsibility and, finally, to stonewalling or the embittered passive resistance that comes from feeling unfairly treated. Indeed, one of the more common forms of destructive criticism in the workplace, says one business consultant, is a blanket, generalized statement like "You're screwing up," delivered in a harsh, sarcastic, angry tone, providing neither a chance to respond nor any suggestion of how to do things better. It leaves the person receiving it feeling helpless and angry.

From the vantage point of emotional intelligence, such criticism displays an ignorance of the feelings it will trigger in those who receive it, and the devastating effect those feelings will have on their motivation, energy, and confidence in doing their work.

This destructive dynamic showed up in a survey of managers who were asked to think back to times they blew up at employees and, in the heat of the moment, made a personal attack.[5] The angry attacks had effects much like they would in a married couple: the employees who received them reacted most often by becoming defensive, making excuses, or evading responsibility. Or they stonewalled — that is, tried to avoid all contact with the manager who blew up at them. The managers were only further annoyed and provoked by these responses, suggesting the beginning of a cycle that, in the business world, ends in the employee quitting or being fired — the business equivalent of a divorce.

Indeed, in a study of 108 managers and white-collar workers, inept criticism was ahead of mistrust, personality struggles, and disputes over power and pay as a reason for conflict on the job.[6] An experiment done at Rensselaer Polytechnic Institute shows just how damaging to working relationships a cutting criticism can be. In a simulation, volunteers were given the task of creating an ad for a new shampoo. Another volunteer (a confederate) supposedly judged the proposed ads; volunteers actually received one of two prearranged criticisms. One critique was considerate and specific. But the other included threats and blamed the person's innate deficiencies, with remarks like, "Didn't even try; can't seem to do anything right" and "Maybe it's just lack of talent. I'd try to get someone else to do it." Understandably, those who were attacked became tense and angry and antagonistic, saying they would refuse to collaborate or cooperate on future projects with the person who gave the criticism. Many indicated they would want to avoid contact altogether — in other words, they felt like stonewalling. The harsh criticism made those who received it so demoralized that they no longer tried as hard at their work and, perhaps most damaging, said they no longer felt capable of doing well. The personal attack was devastating to their morale.

Many managers are too willing to criticize, but frugal with praise, leaving their employees feeling that they only hear about how they're doing when they make a mistake. This propensity to criticism is compounded by managers who delay giving any feedback at all for long periods. "Most problems in an employee's performance are not sudden; they develop slowly overtime," J.R. Larson, a University of Illinois at Urbana psychologist, notes, "When the boss fails to let his feelings be known promptly, it leads to his frustration building up slowly. Then, one day, he blows up about it. If the criticism had been given earlier on, the employee would have been able to correct the problem. Too often people criticize only when things boil over, when they get too angry to contain themselves. And that's when they give the criticism in the worst way, in a tone of biting sarcasm, calling to mind a long list of grievances they had kept to themselves, or making threats. Such attacks backfire. They are received as an affront, so the recipient becomes angry in return. It's the worst way to motivate someone."

THE ARTFUL CRITIQUE

Consider the alternative. An artful critique can be one of the most helpful messages a manager can send. For example, what the contemptuous vice president could have told the software engineer – but did not – was something like: "The main difficulty at this stage is that your plan will take too long and so escalate costs. I'd like you to think more about your proposal, especially the design specifications for software development, to see if you can figure out a way to do the same job more quickly." Such a message has the opposite impact of destructive criticism: instead of creating helplessness, anger, and rebellion, it holds out the hope of doing better and suggests the beginning of a plan for doing so.

An artful critique focuses on what a person has done and can do rather than reading a mark of character into a job poorly done. As Larson observes, "A character attack – calling someone stupid or incompetent – misses the point. You immediately put him on the defensive, so that he's no longer receptive to what you have to tell him about how to do things better." That advice, of course, is precisely the same as for married couples airing their grievances.

And, in terms of motivation, when people believe that their failures are due to some unchangeable deficit in themselves, they lose hope and stop trying. The basic belief that leads to optimism, remember, is that setbacks or failures are due to circumstances that we can do something about to change them for the better.

Harry Levinson, a psychoanalyst turned corporate

consultant, gives the following advice on the art of the critique, which is intricately entwined with the art of praise:

• Be specific. Pick a significant incident, an event that illustrates a key problem that needs changing or a pattern of deficiency, such as the inability to do certain parts of a job well. It demoralizes people just to hear that they are doing "something" wrong without knowing what the specifics are so they can change. Focus on the specifics, saying what the person did well, what was done poorly, and how it could be changed. Don't beat around the bush or be oblique or evasive; it will muddy the real message. This is an "XYZ" statement: say exactly what the problem is, what's wrong with it or how it makes you feel, and what could be changed. "Specificity," Levinson points out, "is just as important for praise as for criticism. I won't say that vague praise has no effect at all, but it doesn't have much, and you can't learn from it.[7]

• Offer a solution. The critique, like all useful feedback, should point to away to fix the problem. Otherwise it leaves the recipient frustrated, demoralized, or demotivated. The critique may open the door to possibilities and alternatives that the person did not realize were there, or simply sensitize her to deficiencies that need attention – but should include suggestions about how to take care of these problems.

• Be present. Critiques, like praise, are most effective face-to-face and in private. People who are uncomfortable giving a criticism – or offering praise – are likely to ease the burden on themselves by doing it at a distance, such as in a memo. But this makes the communication too impersonal, and robs the person receiving it of an opportunity for a response or clarification.

• Be sensitive. This is a call for empathy, for being attuned to the impact of what you say and how you say it on the person at the receiving end. Managers who have little empathy, Levinson points out, are most prone to giving feedback in a hurtful fashion, such as the withering put-down. The net effect of such criticism is destructive: instead of opening the way for a corrective, it creates an emotional backlash of resentment, bitterness, defensiveness, and distance. Levinson also offers some emotional counsel for those at the receiving end of criticism. One is to see the criticism as valuable information about how to do better, not as a personal attack. Another is to watch for the impulse toward defensiveness instead of taking responsibility. And, if it gets too upsetting, ask to resume the meeting later, after a period to absorb the difficult message and cool down a bit. Finally, he advises people to see criticism as an opportunity to work together with the critic to solve the problem, not as an adversarial situation.

— WHAT MAKES A LEADER? —

Adapted from The Harvard Business Review

Every businessperson knows a story about a highly intelligent, highly skilled executive who was promoted into a leadership position only to fail at the job. And they also know a story about someone with solid – but not extraordinary – intellectual abilities and technical skills who was promoted into a similar position and then soared. Such anecdotes support the widespread belief that identifying individuals with the "right stuff" to be leaders is more art than science. After all, the personal styles of superb leaders vary: Some leaders are subdued and analytical; others shout their manifestos from the mountaintops. And just as important, different situations call for different types of leadership. Most mergers need a sensitive negotiator at the helm, whereas many turnarounds require a more forceful authority. I have found, however, that the most effective leaders are alike in one crucial way: they all have a high degree of what has come to be known as emotional intelligence.

It's not that IQ and technical skills are irrelevant. They do matter, but mainly as "threshold capabilities"; that is, they are the entry-level requirements for executive positions. But my research, along with other recent studies, strongly suggests that emotional intelligence is the sine qua non of leadership. Without it, a person can have the best training in the world, an incisive, analytical mind, and an endless supply of smart ideas, but he still won't make a great leader. My colleagues and I have focused on how emotional intelligence operates at work. We have examined the relationship between emotional intelligence and effective performance, especially in leaders. And we have observed how emotional intelligence shows itself on the job. How can you tell if someone has high emotional intelligence, for example, and how can you recognize it in yourself? In the following pages, we'll explore these questions, taking each of the components of emotional intelligence – self-awareness, self-regulation, empathy, and social skill – in turn.

Most large companies today have employed trained psychologists to develop what are known as "competency models" to aid them in identifying, training, and promoting likely stars in the leadership firmament. The psychologists have also developed such models for lower-level positions. While writing *Working With Emotional Intelligence*, I analyzed competency models from 188 companies, most of which were large and global, as well as government agencies. In carrying out this work, my objective was to determine which personal capabilities drove outstanding performance within these organizations, and to what degree they did so. I grouped capabilities into three categories: purely technical skills like accounting and business planning; cognitive abilities like analytical reasoning; and competencies demonstrating emotional intelligence, such as the ability to work with others and effectiveness in leading change. To create some of the competency models, psychologists asked senior managers at the companies to identify the capabilities that typified the organization's most outstanding leaders. To create other models, the psychologists used objective criteria, such as a division's profitability, to differentiate the star performers at senior levels within their organizations from the average ones. Those individuals were then extensively interviewed and tested, and their capabilities were compared. This process resulted in the creation of lists of ingredients for highly effective leaders. The lists ranged in length from 7 to 15 items and included such ingredients as initiative and strategic vision. Some of the competencies reflected purely cognitive, IQ-type abilities, or purely technical skills, while others were based largely on emotional intelligence abilities like self-management.

When I analyzed all this data, I found dramatic results. To be sure, intellect was a driver of outstanding performance. Cognitive skills such as big-picture thinking and long-term vision were particularly important. But when I calculated the ratio of technical skills and IQ to emotional intelligence as ingredients of excellent performance, emotional intelligence proved to be twice as important as the others for jobs at all levels. Moreover, my analysis showed that emotional intelligence played an increasingly important role at the highest levels of the company, where differences in technical skills were of negligible importance.

In other words, the higher the rank of a person considered to be a star performer, the more emotional intelligence capabilities showed up as the reason for his or her effectiveness. When I compared star performers with average ones in senior leadership positions, nearly 90 percent of the competencies that distinguished outstanding performers was attributable to emotional intelligence factors rather than purely cognitive abilities. Other researchers have confirmed that emotional intelligence not only distinguishes outstanding leaders but can also be linked to strong performance.

The findings of the late David McClelland, the renowned researcher in human and organizational behavior, are a good example. In a 1996 study of a global food and beverage company, McClelland found that when senior managers had a critical mass of emotional intelligence capabilities, their divisions outperformed yearly earnings goals by 20 percent. Meanwhile, division leaders without that critical mass underperformed by almost the same amount. McClelland's findings, interestingly, held as true in the company's U.S. divisions as in its divisions in Asia and Europe. In short, the numbers tell us a persuasive story about the link between a company's success and the emotional intelligence of its leaders. And just as important, research is also demonstrating that people can, if they take the right approach, develop their emotional intelligence.

SELF-AWARENESS

Self-awareness is the first component of emotional intelligence – which makes sense when one considers that the Delphic oracle gave the advice to "know thyself" thousands of years ago. Self-awareness means having a deep understanding of one's emotions, strengths, weaknesses, needs, and drives. People with strong self-awareness are neither overly critical nor unrealistically hopeful. Rather, they are honest with themselves and with others. People who have a high degree of self-awareness recognize how their feelings affect them, other people, and their job performance. Thus, a self-aware person who knows that tight deadlines bring out the worst in him plans his time carefully and gets his work done well in advance. Another person with high self-awareness will be able to work with a demanding client. She will understand the client's impact on her moods and the deeper reasons for her frustration. "Their trivial demands take us away from the real work that needs to be done," she might explain. And she will go one step further and turn her anger into something constructive.

Self-awareness extends to a person's understanding of his or her values and goals. Someone who is highly self-aware knows where he is headed and why; so, for example, he will be able to be firm in turning down a job offer that is tempting financially but does not fit with his principles or long-term goals. A person who lacks self-awareness is apt to make decisions that bring on inner turmoil by treading on buried values. "The money looked good so I signed on," someone might say two years into a job, "but the work means so little to me that I'm constantly bored." The decisions of self-aware people mesh with their values; consequently, they often find work to be energizing.

How can one recognize self-awareness? First and foremost, it shows itself as candor and an ability to assess oneself realistically. People with high self-awareness are able to speak accurately and openly – although not necessarily effusively or confessionally –

about their emotions and the impact they have on their work. For instance, one manager I know of was skeptical about a new personal-shopper service that her company, a major department-store chain, was about to introduce. Without prompting from her team or her boss, she offered them an explanation: "It's hard for me to get behind the rollout of this service," she admitted, "because I really wanted to run the project, but I wasn't selected. Bear with me while I deal with that." The manager did indeed examine her feelings; a week later, she was supporting the project fully. Such self-knowledge often shows itself in the hiring process. Ask a candidate to describe a time he got carried away by his feelings and did something he later regretted. Self-aware candidates will be frank in admitting to failure and will often tell their tales with a smile. One of the hallmarks of self-awareness is a self-deprecating sense of humor.

Self-awareness can also be identified during performance reviews. Self-aware people know and are comfortable talking about their limitations and strengths, and they often demonstrate a thirst for constructive criticism. By contrast, people with low self-awareness interpret the message that they need to improve as a threat or a sign of failure. Self-aware people can also be recognized by their self-confidence. They have a firm grasp of their capabilities and are less likely to set themselves up to fail by, for example, overstretching on assignments. They know, too, when to ask for help. And the risks they take on the job are calculated. They won't ask for a challenge that they know they can't handle alone. They'll play to their strengths.

Consider the actions of a midlevel employee who was invited to sit in on a strategy meeting with her company's top executives. Although she was the most junior person in the room, she did not sit there quietly, listening in awestruck or fearful silence. She knew she had a head for clear logic and the skill to present ideas persuasively, and she offered cogent suggestions about the company's strategy. At the same time, her self-awareness stopped her from wandering into territory where she knew she was weak. Despite the value of having self-aware people in the workplace, my research indicates that senior executives don't often give self-awareness the credit it deserves when they look for potential leaders. Many executives mistake candor about feelings for "wimpiness" and fail to give due respect to employees who openly acknowledge their shortcomings. Such people are too readily dismissed as "not tough enough" to lead others.

In fact, the opposite is true. In the first place, people generally admire and respect candor. Furthermore, leaders are constantly required to make judgment calls that require a candid assessment of capabilities – their own and those of others. Do we have the management expertise to acquire a competitor? Can we launch a new product within six months? People who assess themselves honestly – that is, self-aware people – are well suited to do the same for the organizations they run.

SELF-MANAGEMENT

Biological impulses drive our emotions. We cannot do away with them – but we can do much to manage them. Self-regulation, which is like an ongoing inner conversation, is the component of emotional intelligence that frees us from being prisoners of our feelings. People engaged in such a conversation feel bad moods and emotional impulses just as everyone else does, but they find ways to control them and even to channel them in useful ways. Imagine an executive who has just watched a team of his employees present a botched analysis to the company's board of directors. In the gloom that follows, the executive might find himself tempted to pound on the table in anger or kick over a chair. He could leap up and scream at the group. Or he might maintain a grim silence, glaring at everyone before stalking off. But if he had a gift for self-regulation, he would choose a different approach. He would pick his words carefully, acknowledging the team's poor performance without rushing to any hasty judgment. He would then step back to consider the reasons for the failure.

Are they personal — a lack of effort? Are there any mitigating factors? What was his role in the debacle? After considering these questions, he would call the team together, lay out the incident's consequences, and offer his feelings about it. He would then present his analysis of the problem and a well-considered solution.

Why does self-regulation matter so much for leaders? First of all, people who are in control of their feelings and impulses — that is, people who are reasonable — are able to create an environment of trust and fairness. In such an environment, politics and infighting are sharply reduced and productivity is high. Talented people flock to the organization and aren't tempted to leave. And self-regulation has a trickle-down effect. No one wants to be known as a hothead when the boss is known for her calm approach. Fewer bad moods at the top mean fewer throughout the organization. Second, self-regulation is important for competitive reasons. Everyone knows that business today is rife with ambiguity and change. Companies merge and break apart regularly. Technology transforms work at a dizzying pace. People who have mastered their emotions are able to roll with the changes. When a new program is announced, they don't panic; instead, they are able to suspend judgment, seek out information, and listen to the executives as they explain the new program. As the initiative moves forward, these people are able to move with it. Sometimes they even lead the way.

Consider the case of a manager at a large manufacturing company. Like her colleagues, she had used a certain software program for five years. The program drove how she collected and reported data and how she thought about the company's strategy. One day, senior executives announced that a new program was to be installed that would radically change how information was gathered and assessed within the organization. While many people in the company complained bitterly about how disruptive the change would be, the manager mulled over the reasons for the new program and was convinced of its potential to improve performance. She eagerly attended training sessions — some of her colleagues refused to do so — and was eventually promoted to run several divisions, in part because she used the new technology so effectively.

I want to push the importance of self-regulation to leadership even further and make the case that it enhances integrity, which is not only a personal virtue but also an organizational strength. Many of the bad things that happen in companies are a function of impulsive behavior. People rarely plan to exaggerate profits, pad expense accounts, dip into the till, or abuse power for selfish ends. Instead, an opportunity presents itself, and people with low impulse control just say yes. By contrast, consider the behavior of the senior executive at a large food company. The executive was scrupulously honest in his negotiations with local distributors. He would routinely lay out his cost structure in detail, thereby giving the distributors a realistic understanding of the company's pricing. This approach meant the executive couldn't always drive a hard bargain. Now, on occasion, he felt the urge to increase profits by withholding information about the company's costs. But he challenged that impulse — he saw that it made more sense in the long run to counteract it. His emotional self-regulation paid off in strong, lasting relationships with distributors that benefited the company more than any short-term financial gains would have.

The signs of emotional self-regulation, therefore, are easy to see: a propensity for reflection and thoughtfulness; comfort with ambiguity and change; and integrity — an ability to say no to impulsive urges. Like self-awareness, self-regulation often does not get its due. People who can master their emotions are sometimes seen as cold fish their considered responses are taken as a lack of passion. People with fiery temperaments are frequently thought of as "classic" leaders their outbursts are considered hallmarks of charisma and power. But when such people make it to the top, their impulsiveness often works against them. In my research, extreme displays of negative emotion have never emerged as a driver of good leadership.

If there is one trait that virtually all effective leaders have, it is motivation – a variety of self-management where we mobilize our positive emotions to drive us toward our goals. Motivated leaders are driven to achieve beyond expectations – their own and everyone else's. The key word here is achieve. Plenty of people are motivated by external factors, such as a big salary or the status that comes from having an impressive title or being part of a prestigious company. By contrast, those with leadership potential are motivated by a deeply embedded desire to achieve for the sake of achievement. If you are looking for leaders, how can you identify people who are motivated by the drive to achieve rather than by external rewards? The first sign is a passion for the work itself – such people seek out creative challenges, love to learn, and take great pride in a job well done. They also display an unflagging energy to do things better. People with such energy often seem restless with the status quo. They are persistent with their questions about why things are done one way rather than another; they are eager to explore new approaches to their work.

A cosmetics company manager, for example, was frustrated that he had to wait two weeks to get sales results from people in the field. He finally tracked down an automated phone system that would beep each of his salespeople at 5 pm every day. An automated message then prompted them to punch in their number to show how many calls and sales they had made that day. The system shortened the feedback time on sales results from weeks to hours. That story illustrates two other common traits of people who are driven to achieve. They are forever raising the performance bar, and they like to keep score.

Take the performance bar first. During performance reviews, people with high levels of motivation might ask to be "stretched" by their superiors. Of course, an employee who combines self-awareness with internal motivation will recognize her limits – but she won't settle for objectives that seem too easy to fulfill. And it follows naturally that people who are driven to do better also want a way of tracking progress – their own, their team's, and their company's. Whereas people with low achievement motivation are often fuzzy about results, those with high achievement motivation often keep score by tracking such hard measures as profitability or market share. Interestingly, people with high motivation remain optimistic even when the score is against them. In such cases, self-regulation combines with achievement motivation to overcome the frustration and depression that come after a setback or failure.

EMPATHY

Of all the dimensions of emotional intelligence, empathy is the most easily recognized. We have all felt the empathy of a sensitive teacher or friend; we have all been struck by its absence in an unfeeling coach or boss. But when it comes to business, we rarely hear people praised, let alone rewarded, for their empathy. The very word seems unbusinesslike, out of place amid the tough realities of the marketplace. But empathy doesn't mean a kind of "I'm OK, you're OK" mushiness. For a leader, that is, it doesn't mean adopting other people's emotions as one's own and trying to please everybody. That would be a nightmare – it would make action impossible. Rather, empathy means thoughtfully considering employees' feelings – along with other factors – in the process of making intelligent decisions. For an example of empathy in action, consider what happened when two giant brokerage companies merged, creating redundant jobs in all their divisions. One division manager called his people together and gave a gloomy speech that emphasized the number of people who would soon be fired. The manager of another division gave his people a different kind of speech. He was up-front about his own worry and confusion, and he promised to keep people informed and to treat everyone fairly. The difference between these two managers was empathy. The first manager was too worried about his own fate to consider the feelings of his anxiety-stricken colleagues. The second knew intuitively what his people were feeling, and he acknowledged their fears with his words. Is it any surprise that the first manager saw his division sink as many demoralized people, especially the most talented, departed? By contrast, the second manager continued to be a strong leader, his best people stayed, and his division remained as productive as ever.

Empathy is particularly important today as a component of leadership for at least three reasons: the increasing use of teams; the rapid pace of globalization; and the growing need to retain talent. Consider the challenge of leading a team. As anyone who has ever been a part of one can attest, teams are cauldrons of bubbling emotions. They are often charged with reaching a consensus – which is hard enough with two people and much more difficult as the numbers increase. Even in groups with as few as four or five members, alliances form and clashing agendas get set. A team's leader must be able to sense and understand the viewpoints of everyone around the table. That's exactly what a marketing manager at a large information technology company was able to do when she was appointed to lead a troubled team. The group was in turmoil, overloaded by work and missing deadlines. Tensions were high among the members. Tinkering with procedures was not enough to bring the group together and make it an effective part of the company. So the manager took several steps. In a series of one-on-one sessions, she took the time to listen to everyone in the group – what was frustrating them, how they rated their colleagues, whether they felt they had been ignored. And then she directed the team in a way that brought it together: She encouraged people to speak more openly about their frustrations, and she helped people raise constructive complaints during meetings. In short, her empathy allowed her to understand her team's emotional makeup. The result was not just heightened collaboration among members but also added business, as the team was called on for help by a wider range of internal clients.

Globalization is another reason for the rising importance of empathy for business leaders. Cross-cultural dialogue can easily lead to miscues and misunderstandings. Empathy is an antidote. People who have it are attuned to subtleties in body language; they can hear the message beneath the words being spoken. Beyond that, they have a deep understanding of both the existence and the importance of cultural and ethnic differences. Consider the case of an American consultant whose team had just pitched a project to a potential Japanese client. In its dealings with Americans, the team was accustomed to being bombarded with questions after such a proposal, but this time it was greeted with a long silence. Other members of the team, taking the silence as disapproval, were ready to pack and leave. The lead consultant gestured them to stop. Although he was not particularly familiar with Japanese culture, he read the client's face and posture and sensed not rejection but interest — even deep consideration. He was right: when the client finally spoke, it was to give the consulting firm the job.

Finally, empathy plays a key role in the retention of talent, particularly in today's information economy. Leaders have always needed empathy to develop and keep good people, but today the stakes are higher. When good people leave, they take the company's knowledge with them. That's where coaching and mentoring come in. It has repeatedly been shown that coaching and mentoring pay off not just in better performance but also in increased job satisfaction and decreased turnover. But what makes coaching and mentoring work best is the nature of the relationship. Outstanding coaches and mentors get inside the heads of the people they are helping. They sense how to give effective feedback. They know when to push for better performance and when to hold back. In the way they motivate their protégés, they demonstrate empathy in action. In what is probably sounding like a refrain, let me repeat that empathy doesn't get much respect in business. People wonder how leaders can make hard decisions if they are "feeling" for all the people who will be affected. But leaders with empathy do more than sympathize with people around them: They use their knowledge to improve their companies in subtle but important ways.

SOCIAL SKILL

The first two components of emotional intelligence are self-management skills. The last two, empathy and social skill, concern a person's ability to manage relationships with others. As a component of emotional intelligence, social skill is not as simple as it sounds. It's not just a matter of friendliness, although people with high levels of social skill are rarely mean-spirited. Social skill, rather, is friendliness with a purpose: moving people in the direction you desire, whether that's agreement on a new marketing strategy or enthusiasm about a new product.

Socially skilled people tend to have a wide circle of acquaintances, and they have a knack for finding common ground with people of all kinds – a knack for building rapport. That doesn't mean they socialize continually; it means they work according to the assumption that nothing important gets done alone. Such people have a network in place when the time for action comes. Social skill is the culmination of the other dimensions of emotional intelligence. People tend to be very effective at managing relationships when they can understand and control their own emotions and can empathize with the feelings of others.

Even motivation contributes to social skill. Remember that people who are driven to achieve tend to be optimistic, even in the face of setbacks or failure. When people are upbeat, their "glow" is cast upon conversations and other social encounters. They are popular, and for good reason. Because it is the outcome of the other dimensions of emotional intelligence, social skill is recognizable on the job in many ways that will by now sound familiar. Socially skilled people, for instance, are adept at managing teams – that's their empathy at work. Likewise, they are expert persuaders – a manifestation of self-awareness, self-regulation, and empathy combined. Given those skills, good persuaders know when to make an emotional plea, for instance, and when an appeal to reason will work better. And motivation, when publicly visible, makes such people excellent collaborators; their passion for the work spreads to others, and they are driven to find solutions.

But sometimes social skill shows itself in ways the other emotional intelligence components do not. For instance, socially skilled people may at times appear not to be working while at work. They seem to be idly schmoozing – chatting in the hallways with colleagues or joking around with people who are not even connected to their "real" jobs. Socially skilled people, however, don't think it makes sense to arbitrarily limit the scope of their relationships. They build bonds widely because they know that in these fluid times, they may need help someday from people they are just getting to know today.

For example, consider the case of an executive in the strategy department of a global computer manufacturer. By 1993, he was convinced that the company's future lay with the Internet. Over the course of the next year, he found kindred spirits and used his social skill to stitch together a virtual community that cut across levels, divisions, and nations. He then used this de facto team to put up a corporate Web site, among the first by a major company. And, on his own initiative, with no budget or formal status, he signed up the company to participate in an annual Internet industry convention. Calling on his allies and persuading various divisions to donate funds, he recruited more than 50 people from a dozen different units to represent the company at the convention. Management took notice: within a year of the conference, the executive's team formed the basis for the company's first Internet division, and he was formally put in charge of it. To get there, the executive had ignored conventional boundaries, forging and maintaining connections with people in every corner of the organization.

Is social skill considered a key leadership capability in most companies? The answer is yes, especially when compared with the other components of emotional intelligence. People seem to know intuitively that leaders need to manage relationships effectively; no leader is an island. After all, the leader's task is to get work done through other people, and social skill makes that possible. A leader who cannot express her empathy may as well not have it at all. And a leader's motivation will be useless if he cannot communicate his passion to the organization. Social skill allows leaders to put their emotional intelligence to work.

It would be foolish to assert that good-old fashioned IQ and technical ability are not important ingredients in strong leadership. But the recipe would not be complete without emotional intelligence. It was once thought that the components of emotional intelligence were "nice to have" in business leaders. But now we know that, for the sake of performance, these are ingredients that leaders "need to have." It is fortunate, then, that emotional intelligence can be learned. The process is not easy. It takes time and, most of all, commitment. But the benefits that come from having a well-developed emotional intelligence, both for the individual and for the organization, make it worth the effort.

— LEADERSHIP THAT GETS — RESULTS

Adapted From The Harvard Business Review

Ask any group of businesspeople the question "What do effective leaders do?" and you'll hear a sweep of answers. Leaders set strategy; they motivate; they create a mission; they build a culture.

Then ask "What should leaders do?" If the group is seasoned, you'll likely hear one response: the leader's singular job is to get results.

But how? The mystery of what leaders can and ought to do in order to spark the best performance from their people is age-old. Still, effective leadership eludes many people and organizations. One reason is that until recently, virtually no quantitative research has demonstrated which precise leadership behaviors yield positive results.

Leadership experts proffer advice based on inference, experience, and instinct. Sometimes that advice is right on target; sometimes it's not.

Research by the consulting firm Hay/McBer, which draws on a random sample of 3,871 executives selected from a database of more than 20,000 executives worldwide, takes much of the mystery out of effective leadership. The research found six distinct leadership styles, each springing from different components of emotional intelligence. The styles, taken individually, appear to have a direct and unique impact on the working atmosphere of a company, division, or team, and in turn, on its financial performance. And perhaps most important, the research indicates that leaders with the best results do not rely on only one leadership style; they use many or most of them in a given week – seamlessly and in different measure – depending on the business situation.

Imagine the styles, then, as the array of clubs in a golf pro's bag. Over the course of a game, the pro picks and chooses clubs based on the demands of the shot. Sometimes he has to ponder his selection, but usually it is automatic. The pro senses the challenge ahead, swiftly pulls out the right tool, and elegantly puts it to work. That's how high-impact leaders operate, too.

What are the six styles of leadership? Each style, by name and brief description alone, will likely resonate with anyone who leads, is led, or as is the case with most of us, does both. Authoritative leaders mobilize people toward a vision. Affiliative leaders create emotional bonds and harmony. Democratic leaders build consensus through participation. Pacesetting leaders expect excellence and self-direction. Coaching leaders develop people for the future. And coercive leaders demand immediate compliance.

Close your eyes and you can surely imagine a colleague who uses any one of these styles. You most likely use at least one yourself. What is new in this research, then, is its implications for action. First, it offers a fine-grained understanding of how different leadership styles affect performance and results. Second, it offers clear guidance on when a manager should switch between them. It also strongly suggests that switching flexibly is well advised. New, too, is the research's finding that each leadership style springs from different components of emotional intelligence.

MEASURING LEADERSHIP'S IMPACT ├───────────

The late David McClelland, a noted Harvard University psychologist found that leaders with strengths in a critical mass of six or more emotional intelligence competencies were far more effective than peers who lacked such strengths. For instance, when he analyzed the performance of division heads at a global food and beverage company, he found that among leaders with this critical mass of competence, 87 percent placed in the top third for annual salary bonuses based on their business performance. More telling, their divisions on average outperformed yearly revenue targets by 15 to 20 percent.

Those executives who lacked emotional intelligence were rarely rated as outstanding in their annual performance reviews, and their divisions underperformed by an average of almost 20 percent. The research on leadership styles set out to gain a more molecular view of the links among leadership and emotional intelligence, and climate and performance. A team of McClelland's colleagues headed by Mary Fontaine and Ruth Jacobs from what is now the McClelland Institute at the Boston office of HayGroup studied data about or observed thousands of executives, noting specific behaviors and their impact on climate.

How did each individual motivate direct reports? Manage change initiatives? Handle crises? It was a later phase of the research that identified how emotional intelligence capabilities drive the six leadership styles. How does he rate in terms of self-control and social skill? Does a leader show high or low levels of empathy? The team tested each executive's immediate sphere of influence for its climate.

"Climate" is not an amorphous term. First defined by psychologists George Litwin and Richard Stringer and later refined by McClelland and his colleagues, it refers to six key factors that influence an organization's working environment: its flexibility – that is, how free employees feel to innovate unencumbered by red tape; their sense of responsibility to the organization; the level of standards that people set; the sense of accuracy about performance feedback and aptness of rewards; the clarity people have about mission and values; and finally, the level of commitment to a common purpose. All six leadership styles have a measurable effect on each aspect of climate.

Further, when the team looked at the impact of climate on financial results – such as return on sales, revenue growth, efficiency, and profitability – they found a direct correlation between the two. Leaders who used styles that positively affected the climate had decidedly better financial results than those who did not. That is not to say that organizational climate is the only driver of performance. Economic conditions and competitive dynamics matter enormously. But this analysis strongly suggests that climate accounts for nearly a third of results. And that's simply too much of an impact to ignore.

Executives use six main leadership styles, but only four of the six consistently have a positive effect on climate and results. Let's look then at each style of leadership in detail, starting with the Authoritative (or Visionary) Style.

THE AUTHORITATIVE STYLE   ⊢————————

Tom was the vice-president of marketing at a floundering national restaurant chain that specialized in pizza. Needless to say, the company's poor performance troubled the senior managers, but they were at a loss for what to do. Every Monday, they met to review recent sales, struggling to come up with fixes. To Tom, the approach didn't make sense. "We were always trying to figure out why our sales were down last week. We had the whole company looking backward instead of figuring out what we had to do tomorrow."

Tom saw an opportunity to change people's way of thinking at an off-site strategy meeting. There, the conversation began with stale truisms: the company had to drive up shareholder wealth and increase return on assets. Tom believed those concepts didn't have the power to inspire a restaurant manager to be innovative or to do better than a good-enough job.

So Tom made a bold move. In the middle of a meeting, he made an impassioned plea for his colleagues to think from the customer's perspective. Customers want convenience, he said. The company was not in the restaurant business, it was in the business of distributing high quality, convenient-to-get pizza. That notion and nothing else should drive everything the company did.

With his vibrant enthusiasm and clear vision – the hallmarks of the authoritative style – Tom filled a leadership vacuum at the company. Indeed, his concept became the core of the new mission statement. But this conceptual breakthrough was just the beginning. Tom made sure that the mission statement was built into the company's strategic planning process as the designated driver of growth. And he ensured that the vision was articulated so that local restaurant managers understood they were the key to the company's success and were free to find new ways to distribute pizza.

Changes came quickly. Within weeks, many local managers started guaranteeing fast, new delivery times. Even better, they started to act like entrepreneurs, finding ingenious locations to open new branches: kiosks on busy street corners and in bus and train stations, even from carts in airports and hotel lobbies.

Tom's success was no fluke. The research indicates that of the six leadership styles, the authoritative one is most effective, driving up every aspect of climate. Take clarity. The authoritative leader is a visionary; he motivates people by making clear to them how their work fits into a larger vision for the organization. People who work for such leaders understand that what they do matters and why.

Authoritative leadership also maximizes commitment to the organization's goals and strategy. By framing the individual tasks within a grand vision, the authoritative leader defines standards that revolve around that vision. When he gives performance feedback – whether positive or negative – the singular criterion is whether or not that performance furthers the vision. The standards for success are clear to all, as are the rewards.

Finally, consider the style's impact on flexibility. An

authoritative leader states the end but generally gives people plenty of leeway to devise their own means. Authoritative leaders give people the freedom to innovate, experiment, and take calculated risks. Because of its positive impact, the authoritative style works well in almost any business situation. But it is particularly effective when a business is adrift. An authoritative leader charts a new course and sells his people on a fresh long-term vision.

The authoritative style, powerful though it may be, will not work in every situation. The approach fails, for instance, when a leader is working with a team of experts or peers who are more experienced than he is; they may see the leader as pompous or out-of-touch. Another limitation: if a manager trying to be authoritative becomes overbearing, he can undermine the egalitarian spirit of an effective team. Yet even with such caveats, leaders would be wise to grab for the authoritative "club" more often than not. It may not guarantee a hole in one, but it certainly helps with the long drive.

THE COACHING STYLE

A product unit at a global computer company had seen sales plummet from twice as much as its competitors to only half as much. So Lawrence, the president of the manufacturing division, decided to close the unit and reassign its people and products. Upon hearing the news, James, the head of the doomed unit, decided to go over his boss's head and plead his case to the CEO. What did Lawrence do? Instead of blowing up at James, he sat down with his rebellious direct report and talked over not just the decision to close the division but also James's future. He explained to James how moving to another division would help him develop new skills. It would make him a better leader and teach him more about the company's business. Lawrence acted more like a counselor than a traditional boss.

He listened to James's concerns and hopes, and he shared his own. He said he believed James had grown stale in his current job; it was, after all, the only place he'd worked in the company. He predicted that James would blossom in a new role. The conversation then took a practical turn. James had not yet had his meeting with the CEO – the one he had impetuously demanded when he heard of his division's closing. Knowing this – and also knowing that the CEO unwaveringly supported the closing – Lawrence took the time to coach James on how to present his case in that meeting. "You don't get an audience with the CEO very often," he noted, "let's make sure you impress him with your thoughtfulness."

He advised James not to plead his personal case but to focus on the business unit: "If he thinks you're in there for your own glory, he'll throw you out faster than you walked through the door." And he urged him to put his ideas in writing; the CEO always appreciated that.

Lawrence's reason for coaching instead of scolding? "James is a good guy, very talented and promising," the executive explained to us, "and I don't want this to derail his career. I want him to stay with the company, I want him to work out, I want him to learn, I want him to benefit and grow. Just because he screwed up doesn't mean he's terrible."

Lawrence's actions illustrate the coaching style par excellence. Coaching leaders help employees identify their unique strengths and weaknesses and tie them to their personal and career aspirations. They encourage employees to establish long-term development goals and help them conceptualize a plan for attaining them. They make agreements with their employees about their role and responsibilities in enacting development plans, and they give plentiful instruction and feedback.

Coaching leaders excel at delegating; they give employees challenging assignments, even if that means the tasks won't be accomplished quickly. In other words, these leaders are willing to put up with short-term failure if it furthers long-term learning.

Of the six styles, our research found that the coaching style is used least often. Many leaders told us they don't have the time in this high-pressure economy for the slow and tedious work of teaching people and helping them grow. But after a first session, it takes little or no extra time. Leaders who ignore this style are passing up a powerful tool: its impact on climate and performance are markedly positive.

Admittedly, there is a paradox in coaching's positive effect on business performance because coaching focuses primarily on personal development, not on immediate work-related tasks. Even so, coaching improves results. The reason: it requires constant dialogue, and that dialogue has a way of pushing up every driver of climate. Take flexibility. When an employee knows his boss watches him and cares about what he does, he feels free to experiment. After all, he's sure to get quick and constructive feedback.

Similarly, the ongoing dialogue of coaching guarantees that people know what is expected of them and how their work fits into a larger vision or strategy. That affects responsibility and clarity. As for commitment, coaching helps there, too, because the style's implicit message is, "I believe in you, I'm investing in you, and I expect your best efforts." Employees very often rise to that challenge with their heart, mind, and soul.

The coaching style works well in many business situations, but it is perhaps most effective when people on the receiving end are "up for it." For instance, the coaching style works particularly well when employees are already aware of their weaknesses and would like to improve their performance. Similarly, the style works well when employees realize how cultivating new abilities can help them advance. In short, it works best with employees who want to be coached.

By contrast, the coaching style makes little sense when employees, for whatever reason, are resistant to learning or changing their ways. And it flops if the leader lacks the expertise to help the employee along. The fact is, many managers are unfamiliar with or simply inept at coaching, particularly when it comes to giving ongoing performance feedback that motivates rather than creates fear or apathy.

Some companies have realized the positive impact of the style and are trying to make it a core competence. At some companies, a significant portion of annual bonuses are tied to an executive's development of his or her direct reports. But many organizations have yet to take full advantage of this leadership style. Although the coaching style may not scream "bottom-line results," it delivers them.

THE AFFILIATIVE STYLE

If the authoritative leader urges, "Come with me," the affiliative leader says, "People come first." This leadership style revolves around people – its proponents value individuals and their emotions more than tasks and goals. The affiliative leader strives to keep employees happy and to create harmony among them. He manages by building strong emotional bonds and then reaping the benefits of such an approach, namely fierce loyalty.

The style also has a markedly positive effect on communication. People who like one another a lot talk a lot. They share ideas; they share inspiration. And the style drives up flexibility; friends trust one another, allowing habitual innovation and risk taking. Flexibility also rises because the affiliative leader, like a parent who adjusts household rules for a maturing adolescent, doesn't impose unnecessary strictures on how employees get their work done. They give people the freedom to do their job in the way they think is most effective.

As for a sense of recognition and reward for work well done, the affiliative leader offers ample positive feedback. Such feedback has special potency in the workplace because it is all too rare: outside of an annual review, most people usually get no feedback on their day-today efforts–or only negative feedback. That makes the affiliative leader's positive words all the more motivating.

Finally, affiliative leaders are masters at building a sense of belonging. They are, for instance, likely to take their direct reports out for a meal or a drink, one-on-one, to see how they're doing. They will bring in a cake to celebrate a group accomplishment. They are natural relationship builders.

Joe Torre, at one time the heart and soul of the New York Yankees, was a classic affiliative leader. During the 1999 World Series, Torre tended ably to the psyches of his players as they endured the emotional pressure cooker of a pennant race. All season long, he made a special point to praise Scott Brosius, whose father had died during the season, for staying committed even as he mourned.

At the celebration party after the team's final game, Torre specifically sought out right fielder Paul O'Neill. Although he had received the news of his father's death that morning, O'Neill chose to play in the decisive game – and he burst into tears the moment it ended. Torre made a point of acknowledging O'Neill's personal struggle, calling him a "warrior." Torre also used the spotlight of the victory celebration to praise two players whose return the following year was threatened by contract disputes. In doing so, he sent a clear message to the team and to the club's owner that he valued the players immensely – too much to lose them.

Along with ministering to the emotions of his people, an affiliative leader may also tend to his own emotions openly. The year his brother was near death awaiting a heart transplant, Torre shared his worries with his players. He also spoke candidly with the team about his treatment for prostate cancer. The affiliative style's generally positive impact makes it a good all-weather approach, but leaders should employ it particularly when trying to build team harmony, increase morale, improve communication, or repair broken trust.

For instance, one executive was hired to replace a ruthless team leader. The former leader had taken credit for his employees' work and had attempted to pit them against one another. His efforts ultimately failed, but the team he left behind was suspicious and weary. The new executive managed to mend the situation by unstintingly showing emotional honesty and rebuilding ties. Several months in, her leadership had created a renewed sense of commitment and energy.

Despite its benefits, the affiliative style should not be used alone. Its exclusive focus on praise can allow poor performance to go uncorrected; employees may perceive that mediocrity is tolerated. And because affiliative leaders rarely offer constructive advice on how to improve, employees must figure out how to do so on their own. When people need clear directives to navigate through complex challenges, the affiliative style leaves them rudderless.

Indeed, if overly relied on, this style can actually steer a group to failure. Perhaps that is why many affiliative leaders, including Torre, use this style in close conjunction with the authoritative style. Authoritative leaders state a vision, set standards, and let people know how their work is furthering the group's goals. Alternate that with the caring, nurturing approach of the affiliative leader, and you have a potent combination.

THE DEMOCRATIC STYLE

Sister Mary ran a Catholic school system in a large metropolitan area. One of the schools – the only private school in an impoverished neighborhood – had been losing money for years, and the archdiocese could no longer afford to keep it open. When Sister Mary eventually got the order to shut it down, she didn't just lock the doors.

She called a meeting of all the teachers and staff at the school and explained to them the details of the financial crisis – the first time anyone working at the school had been included in the business side of the institution. She asked for their ideas on ways to keep the school open and on how to handle the closing, should it come to that. Sister Mary spent much of her time at the meeting just listening. She did the same at later meetings for school parents and for the community and during a successive series of meetings for the school's teachers and staff.

After two months of meetings, the consensus was clear: the school would have to close. A plan was made to transfer students to other schools in the Catholic system. The final outcome was no different than if Sister Mary had gone ahead and closed the school the day she was told to. But by allowing the school's constituents to reach that decision collectively, Sister Mary received none of the backlash that would have accompanied such a move. People mourned the loss of the school, but they understood its inevitability. Virtually no one objected.

Compare that with the experiences of a priest in our research who headed another Catholic school. He, too, was told to shut it down. And he did – by fiat. The result was disastrous: parents filed lawsuits, teachers and parents picketed, and local newspapers ran editorials attacking his decision. It took a year to resolve the disputes before he could finally go ahead and close the school.

Sister Mary exemplifies the democratic style in action – and its benefits. By spending time getting people's ideas and buy-in, a leader builds trust, respect, and commitment. By letting workers themselves have a say in decisions that affect their goals and how they do their work, the democratic leader drives up flexibility and responsibility. And by listening to employees' concerns, the democratic leader learns what to do to keep morale high. Finally, because they have a say in setting their goals and the standards for evaluating success, people operating in a democratic system tend to be very realistic about what can and cannot be accomplished.

However, the democratic style has its drawbacks, which is why its impact on climate is not as high as some of the other styles. One of its more exasperating consequences can be endless meetings where ideas are mulled over, consensus remains elusive, and the only visible result is scheduling more meetings. Some democratic leaders use the style to put off making crucial decisions, hoping that enough thrashing things out will eventually yield a blinding insight. In reality, their people end up feeling confused and leaderless. Such an approach can even escalate conflicts.

When does the style work best? This approach is ideal when a leader is himself uncertain about the best direction to take and needs ideas and guidance from able employees. And even if a leader has a strong vision, the democratic style works well to generate fresh ideas for executing that vision. The democratic style, of course, makes much less sense when employees are not competent or informed enough to offer sound advice. And it almost goes without saying that building consensus is wrongheaded in times of crisis.

Take the case of a CEO whose computer company was severely threatened by changes in the market. He always sought consensus about what to do. As competitors stole customers and customers' needs changed, he kept appointing committees to consider the situation. When the market made a sudden shift because of a new technology, the CEO froze in his tracks.

The board replaced him before he could appoint yet another task force to consider the situation. The new CEO, while occasionally democratic and affiliative, relied heavily on the authoritative style, especially in his first months.

THE PACESETTING STYLE

The pacesetting style has its place in the leader's repertoire, but it should be used sparingly. That's not what we expected to find. After all, the hallmarks of the pacesetting style sound admirable. The leader sets extremely high performance standards and exemplifies them himself. He is obsessive about doing things better and faster, and he asks the same of everyone around him. He quickly pinpoints poor performers and demands more from them. If they don't rise to the occasion, he replaces them with people who can.

You would think such an approach would improve results, but it doesn't. In fact, the pacesetting style destroys climate. Many employees feel overwhelmed by the pacesetter's demands for excellence, and their morale drops. Guidelines for working may be clear in the leader's head, but she does not state them clearly; she expects people to know what to do and even thinks, "If I have to tell you, you're the wrong person for the job." Work becomes not a matter of doing one's best along a clear course so much as second-guessing what the leader wants. At the same time, people often feel that the pacesetter doesn't trust them to work in their own way or to take initiative. Flexibility and responsibility evaporate; work becomes so task focused and routinized it's boring. As for rewards, the pacesetter either gives no feedback on how people are doing or jumps in to take over when he thinks they're lagging. And if the leader should leave, people feel directionless – they're so used to "the expert" setting the rules. Finally, commitment dwindles under the regime of a pacesetting leader because people have no sense of how their personal efforts fit into the big picture.

For an example of the pacesetting style, take the case of Sam, a biochemist in R&D at a large pharmaceutical company. Sam's superb technical expertise made him an early star: he was the one everyone turned to when they needed help. Soon he was promoted to head of a team developing a new product. The other scientists on the team were as competent and self-motivated as Sam; his métier as team leader became offering himself as a model of how to do first-class scientific work under tremendous deadline pressure, pitching in when needed. His team completed its task in record time.

But then came a new assignment: Sam was put in charge of R&D for his entire division. As his tasks expanded and he had to articulate a vision, coordinate projects, delegate responsibility, and help develop others, Sam began to slip. Not trusting that his subordinates were as capable as he was, he became a micromanager, obsessed with details and taking over for others when their performance slackened. Instead of trusting them to improve with guidance and development, Sam found himself working nights and weekends after stepping in to take over for the head of a floundering research team. Finally, his own boss suggested, to his relief, that he return to his old job as head of a product development team.

Although Sam faltered, the pacesetting style isn't always a disaster. The approach works well when all employees are self-motivated, highly competent, and need little direction or coordination – for example, it can work for leaders of highly skilled and self-motivated professionals, like R&D groups or legal teams. And, given a talented team to lead, pacesetting does exactly that: gets work done on time or even ahead of schedule. Yet like any leadership style, pacesetting should never be used by itself.

THE COERCIVE STYLE

A computer company was in crisis mode – its sales and profits were falling, its stock was losing value precipitously, and its shareholders were in an uproar. The board brought in a new CEO with a reputation as a turnaround artist. He set to work chopping jobs, selling off divisions, and making the tough decisions that should have been executed years before. The company was saved, at least in the short-term. From the start, though, the CEO created a reign of terror, bullying and demeaning his executives, roaring his displeasure at the slightest misstep. The company's top echelons were decimated not just by his erratic firings but also by defections. The CEO's direct reports, frightened by his tendency to blame the bearer of bad news, stopped bringing him any news at all. Morale was at an all-time low – a fact reflected in another downturn in the business after the short-term recovery. The CEO was eventually fired by the board of directors.

It's easy to understand why of all the leadership styles, the coercive one is the least effective in most situations. Consider what the style does to an organization's climate. Flexibility is the hardest hit. The leader's extreme top-down decision making kills new ideas on the vine. People feel so disrespected that they think, "I won't even bring my ideas up – they'll only be shot down." Likewise, people's sense of responsibility evaporates: unable to act on their own initiative, they lose their sense of ownership and feel little accountability for their performance. Some become so resentful they adopt the attitude, "I'm not going to help this bastard."

Coercive leadership also has a damaging effect on the rewards system. Most high performing workers are motivated by more than money – they seek the satisfaction of work well done. The coercive style erodes such pride. And finally, the style undermines one of the leader's prime tools – motivating people by showing them how their job fits into a grand, shared mission. Such a loss, measured in terms of diminished clarity and commitment, leaves people alienated from their own jobs, wondering, "How does any of this matter?"

Given the impact of the coercive style, you might assume it should never be applied. The research, however, uncovered a few occasions when it worked masterfully.

Take the case of a division president who was brought in to change the direction of a food company that was losing money. His first act was to have the executive conference room demolished. To him, the room – with its long marble table that looked like "the deck of the Starship Enterprise" – symbolized the tradition-bound formality that was paralyzing the company. The destruction of the room, and the subsequent move to a smaller, more informal setting, sent a message no one could miss, and the division's culture changed quickly in its wake.

That said, the coercive style should be used only with extreme caution and in the few situations when it is absolutely imperative, such as during a turnaround or when a hostile takeover is looming. In those cases, the coercive style can break failed business habits and shock people into new ways of working. It is always appropriate during a genuine emergency, like in the aftermath of an earthquake or a fire. And it can work with problem employees with whom all else has failed.

But if a leader relies solely on this style or continues to use it once the emergency passes, the long-term impact of his insensitivity to the morale and feelings of those he leads will be ruinous.

LEADERS NEED MANY STYLES   ⊢━━━━━━━━━━

Many studies, including this one, have shown that the more styles a leader exhibits, the better. Leaders who have mastered four or more – especially the authoritative, democratic, affiliative, and coaching styles – have the very best climate and business performance. And the most effective leaders switch flexibly among the leadership styles as needed. Although that may sound daunting, we've witnessed it more often than you might guess, at both large corporations and tiny start-ups, by seasoned veterans who could explain exactly how and why they lead and by entrepreneurs who claim to lead by gut alone.

Such leaders don't mechanically match their style to fit a checklist of situations – they are far more fluid. They are exquisitely sensitive to the impact they are having on others and seamlessly adjust their style to get the best results. These are leaders, for example, who can read in the first minutes of conversation that a talented but underperforming employee has been demoralized by an unsympathetic, do-it-the-way-I-tell-you manager and needs to be inspired through a reminder of why her work matters. Or that leader might choose to reenergize the employee by asking her about her dreams and aspirations and finding ways to make her job more challenging. Or that initial conversation might signal that the employee needs an ultimatum: improve or leave.

For an example of fluid leadership in action, consider Joan, the general manager of a major division at a global food and beverage company. Joan was appointed to her job while the division was in a deep crisis. It had not made its profit targets for six years; in the most recent year, it had missed by $50 million. Morale among the top management team was miserable; mistrust and resentments were rampant.

Joan's directive from above was clear: turn the division around. Joan did so with a nimbleness in switching among leadership styles that is rare. From the start, she realized she had a short window to demonstrate effective leadership and to establish rapport and trust. She also knew that she urgently needed to be informed about what was not working, so her first task was to listen to key people.

During her first week on the job she had lunch and dinner meetings with each member of the management team. Joan sought to get each person's understanding of the current situation. But her focus was not so much on learning how each person diagnosed the problem as on getting to know each manager as a person. Here Joan employed the affiliative style: she explored their lives, dreams, and aspirations.

She also stepped into the coaching role, looking for ways she could help the team members achieve what they wanted in their careers. For instance, one manager who had been getting feedback that he was a poor team player confided his worries to her. He thought he was a good team member, but he was plagued by persistent complaints. Recognizing that he was a talented executive and a valuable asset to the company, Joan made an agreement with him to point out (in private) when his actions undermined his goal of being seen as a team player.

She followed the one-on-one conversations with a three-day off-site meeting. Her goal here was team building, so that everyone would own whatever solution for the business problems emerged. Her initial stance at the offsite meeting was that of a democratic leader. She encouraged everyone to express freely their frustrations and complaints.

The next day, Joan had the group focus on solutions: each person made three specific proposals about what needed to be done. As Joan clustered the suggestions, a natural consensus emerged about priorities for the business, such as cutting costs. As the group came up with specific action plans, Joan got the commitment and buy-in she sought.

With that vision in place, Joan shifted into the authoritative style, assigning accountability for each follow-up step to specific executives and holding them responsible for their accomplishment. For example, the division had been dropping prices on products without increasing its volume. One obvious solution was to raise prices, but the previous VP of sales had dithered and had let the problem fester. The new VP of sales now had responsibility to adjust the price points to fix the problem.

Over the following months, Joan's main stance was authoritative. She continually articulated the group's new vision in a way that reminded each member of how his or her role was crucial to achieving these goals. And, especially during the first few weeks of the plan's implementation, Joan felt that the urgency of the business crisis justified an occasional shift into the coercive style should someone fail to meet his or her responsibility. As she put it, "I had to be brutal about this follow-up and make sure this stuff happened. It was going to take discipline and focus."

The results? Every aspect of climate improved. People were innovating. They were talking about the division's vision and crowing about their commitment to new, clear goals. The ultimate proof of Joan's fluid leadership style is written in black ink: after only seven months, her division exceeded its yearly profit target by $5 million.

EXPANDING YOUR REPERTORY

Few leaders, of course, have all six styles in their repertory, and even fewer know when and how to use them. In fact, as these findings have been shown to leaders in many organizations, the most common responses have been, "But I have only two of those!" and, "I can't use all those styles. It wouldn't be natural."

Such feelings are understandable, and in some cases, the antidote is relatively simple. The leader can build a team with members who employ styles she lacks. Take the case of a VP for manufacturing. She successfully ran a global factory system largely by using the affiliative style. She was on the road constantly, meeting with plant managers, attending to their pressing concerns, and letting them know how much she cared about them personally. She left the division's strategy – extreme efficiency – to a trusted lieutenant with a keen understanding of technology, and she delegated its performance standards to a colleague who was adept at the authoritative approach. She also had a pacesetter on her team who always visited the plants with her.

An alternative approach, and one I would recommend more, is for leaders to expand their own style repertories. To do so, leaders must first understand which emotional intelligence competencies underlie the leadership styles they are lacking. They can then work assiduously to increase their quotient of them.

For instance, an affiliative leader has strengths in three emotional intelligence competencies: in empathy, in building relationships, and in communication. Empathy – sensing how people are feeling in the moment – allows the affiliative leader to respond to employees in a way that is highly congruent with that person's emotions, thus building rapport. The affiliative leader also displays a natural ease in forming new relationships, getting to know someone as a person, and cultivating a bond.

Finally, the outstanding affiliative leader has mastered the art of interpersonal communication, particularly in saying just the right thing or making the apt symbolic gesture at just the right moment. So if you are primarily a pacesetting leader who wants to be able to use the affiliative style more often, you would need to improve your level of empathy and, perhaps, your skills at building relationships or communicating effectively.

As another example, an authoritative leader who wants to add the democratic style to his repertory might need to work on the capabilities of collaboration and communication.

Hour to hour, day to day, week to week, executives must play their leadership styles like golf clubs, the right one at just the right time and in the right measure. The payoff is in the results.

LEADERSHIP STYLES

LEADERSHIP STYLE	HOW IT BUILDS RESONANCE	IMPACT ON CLIMATE	WHEN APPROPRIATE
VISIONARY (OR AUTHORITATIVE)	MOVES PEOPLE TOWARD SHARED DREAMS	MOST STRONGLY POSITIVE	WHEN CHANGE REQUIRES A NEW VISION, OR WHEN A CLEAR DIRECTION IS NEEDED
COACHING	CONNECTS WHAT A PERSON WANTS WITH THE TEAM'S GOALS	HIGHLY POSITIVE	TO HELP A PERSON CONTRIBUTE MORE EFFECTIVELY TO THE TEAM
AFFILIATIVE	CREATES HARMONY BY CONNECTING PEOPLE TO EACH OTHER	POSITIVE	TO HEAL RIFTS IN A TEAM, MOTIVATE DURING SUCCESSFUL TIMES, OR STRENGTHEN CONNECTIONS
DEMOCRATIC	VALUES PEOPLE'S INPUT/GETS COMMITMENT THROUGH PARTICIPATION	POSITIVE	TO BUILD BUY IN OR CONSENSUS, OR TO GET VALUABLE INPUT FROM TEAM MEMBERS
PACESETTING	SETS CHALLENGING AND EXCITING GOALS	OFTEN HIGHLY NEGATIVE BECAUSE POORLY EXECUTED	TO GET HIGH QUALITY RESULTS FROM A MOTIVATED AND COMPETENT TEAM
COMMANDNG (OR COERCIVE)	SOOTHES FEARS BY GIVING CLEAR DIRECTION IN AN EMERGENCY	OFTEN HIGHLY NEGATIVE BECAUSE MISUSED	IN CRISIS, TO KICK START A TURNAROUND

THE GROUP IQ

Adapted From Emotional Intelligence

Today's economy is largely driven by knowledge workers, people whose productivity is marked by adding value to information – whether as market analysts, writers, or computer programmers. Peter Drucker, who coined the term "knowledge worker," points out that such workers' expertise is highly specialized and that their productivity depends on their efforts being coordinated as part of an organizational team. Writers are not publishers; computer programmers are not software distributors. While people have always worked in tandem, notes Drucker, with knowledge work, "teams become the work unit rather than the individual himself." And that suggests why emotional intelligence, the skills that help people harmonize, is increasingly valued as a workplace asset in today's economy.

Perhaps the most rudimentary form of organizational teamwork is the meeting, that inescapable part of an executive's lot – in a boardroom, on a conference call, in someone's office. Meetings are but the most obvious, and a somewhat antiquated, example of the sense in which work is shared – as well as through electronic networks, e-mail, teleconferences, work teams, informal networks, and the like. To the degree that the explicit hierarchy as mapped on an organizational chart is the skeleton of an organization, these human touchpoints are its central nervous system.

Whenever people come together to collaborate, whether it be in an executive planning meeting or as a team working toward a shared product, there is a very real sense in which they have a group IQ, the sum total of the talents and skills of all those involved. And how well they accomplish their task will be determined by how high that IQ is. The single most important element in group intelligence, it turns out, is not the average IQ in the academic sense, but rather in terms of emotional intelligence. The key to a high group IQ is social harmony. It is this ability to harmonize that, all other things being equal, will make one group especially talented, productive, and successful, and another – with members whose talent and skill are equal in other regards – do poorly.

The idea that there is a group intelligence at all comes from Robert Sternberg, a Yale psychologist, and Wendy Williams, a former graduate student of his, who were seeking to understand why some groups are far more effective than others.[8] After all, when people come together to work as a group, each brings certain talents – say, a high verbal fluency, creativity, empathy, or technical expertise. While a group can be no "smarter" than the sum total of all these specific strengths, it can be much dumber if its internal workings don't allow people to share their talents.

This maxim became evident when Sternberg and Williams recruited people to take part in groups that were given the creative challenge of coming up with an effective advertising campaign for a fictitious sweetener that showed promise as a sugar substitute.

One surprise was that people who were too eager to take part were a drag on the group, lowering its overall performance; these eager beavers were too controlling or domineering. Such people seemed to lack a basic element of social intelligence, the ability to recognize what is apt and what inappropriate in give-and-take. Another negative was having deadweight, members who did not participate.

The single most important factor in maximizing the excellence of a group's product was the degree to which the members were able to create a state of internal harmony, which lets them take advantage of the full talent of their members. The overall performance of harmonious groups was helped by having a member who was particularly talented; groups with more friction were far less able to capitalize on having members of great ability. In groups where there are high levels of emotional and social static – whether it be from fear or anger, from rivalries or resentments – people cannot offer their best. But harmony allows a group to take maximum advantage of its most creative and talented members' abilities.

While the moral of this tale is quite clear for, say, work teams, it has a more general implication for anyone who works within an organization. Many things people do at work depend on their ability to call on a loose network of fellow workers; different tasks can mean calling on different members of the network. In effect, this creates the chance for ad hoc groups, each with a membership tailored to offer an optimal array of talents, expertise, and placement. Just how well people can "work" a network – in effect, make it into a temporary, ad hoc team – is a crucial factor in on-the-job success.

Consider, for example, a classic study of star performers at Bell Labs, the scientific think tank near Princeton operated by the old AT&T back when it was a telephone monopoly. Such labs are peopled by engineers and scientists who are all at the top on academic IQ tests. But within this pool of talent, some emerge as stars, while others are only average in their output. What makes the difference between stars and the others is not their academic IQ, but their emotional IQ. They are better able to motivate themselves, and better able to work their informal networks into ad hoc teams.

The "stars" were studied in one division at the labs, a unit that creates and designs the electronic switches that control telephone systems – a highly sophisticated and demanding piece of electronic engineering.[9] Because the work is beyond the capacity of any one person to tackle, it is done in teams that can range from just 5 or so engineers to 150. No single engineer knows enough to do the job alone; getting things done demands tapping other people's expertise. To find out what made the difference between those who were highly productive and those who were only average, Robert Kelley and Janet Caplan had managers and peers nominate the 10 to 15 percent of engineers who stood out as stars.

When they compared the stars with everyone else, the most dramatic finding, at first, was the paucity of differences between the two groups. "Based on a wide range of cognitive and social measures, from standard tests for IQ to personality inventories, there's little meaningful difference in innate abilities," Kelley and Caplan wrote in the Harvard Business Review. "As it develops, academic talent was not a good predictor of on-the-job productivity," nor was IQ.

But after detailed interviews, the critical differences emerged in the internal and interpersonal strategies "stars" used to get their work done. One of the most important turned out to be a rapport with a network of key people. Things go more smoothly for the standouts because they put time into cultivating good relationships with people whose services might be needed in a crunch as part of an instant ad hoc team to solve a problem or handle a crisis.

"A middle performer at Bell Labs talked about being stumped by a technical problem," Kelley and Caplan observed. "He painstakingly called various technical gurus and then waited, wasting valuable time while calls went unreturned and e-mail messages unanswered. Star performers, however, rarely face such situations because they do the work of building reliable networks before they actually need them. When they call someone for advice, stars almost always get a faster answer."

Informal networks are especially critical for handling unanticipated problems. "The formal organization is set up to handle easily anticipated problems," one study of these networks observes. "But when unexpected problems arise, the informal organization kicks in. Its complex web of social ties form every time colleagues communicate, and solidify over time into surprisingly stable networks. Highly adaptive, informal networks move diagonally and elliptically, skipping entire functions to get things done."[10]

The analysis of informal networks shows that just because people work together day to day they will not necessarily trust each other with sensitive information (such as a desire to change jobs, or resentment about how a manager or peer behaves), nor turn to them in crisis. Indeed, a more sophisticated view of informal networks shows that there are at least three varieties: communications webs – who talks to whom; expertise networks, based on which people are turned to for advice; and trust networks.

Being a main node in the expertise network means someone will have a reputation for technical excellence, which often leads to a promotion. But there is virtually no relationship between being an expert and being seen as someone people can trust with their secrets, doubts, and vulnerabilities. A petty office tyrant or micromanager may be high on expertise, but will be so low on trust that it will undermine their ability to manage, and effectively exclude them from informal networks. The stars of an organization are often those who have thick connections on all networks, whether communications, expertise, or trust.

Beyond a mastery of these essential networks, other forms of organizational savvy the Bell Labs stars had mastered included effectively coordinating their efforts in teamwork; being leaders in building consensus; being able to see things from the perspective of others, such as customers or others on a work team; persuasiveness; and promoting cooperation while avoiding conflicts. While all of these rely on social skills, the stars also displayed another kind of knack: taking initiative – being self-motivated enough to take on responsibilities above and beyond their stated job – and self-management in the sense of regulating their time and work commitments well. All such skills, of course, are aspects of emotional intelligence.

There are strong signs that what is true at such labs augurs for the future of all corporate life, where the basic skills of emotional intelligence will be ever more important, in teamwork, in cooperation, in helping people learn together how to work more effectively. Knowledge-based services and intellectual capital are central to corporations, and improving the way people work together is a major way to leverage intellectual capital, making a critical competitive difference. To thrive, if not survive, corporations would do well to boost their collective emotional intelligence.

PRIMAL LEADERSHIP

Adapted from Primal Leadership

Great leaders move us. They ignite our passion and inspire the best in us. When we try to explain why they are so effective, we speak of strategy, vision, or powerful ideas. But the reality is much more primal: Great leadership works through the emotions.

No matter what leaders set out to do — whether it's creating strategy or mobilizing teams to action — their success depends on how they do it. Even if they get everything else just right, if leaders fail in this primal task of driving emotions in the right direction, nothing they do will work as well as it could or should.

Consider, for example, a pivotal moment in a news division at the BBC, the British media giant. The division had been set up as an experiment, and while its 200 or so journalists and editors felt they had given their best, management had decided the division would have to close.

It didn't help that the executive sent to deliver the decision to the assembled staff started off with a glowing account of how well rival operations were doing, and that he had just returned from a wonderful trip to Cannes. The news itself was bad enough, but the brusque, even contentious manner of the executive incited something beyond the expected frustration. People became enraged — not just at the management decision, but also at the bearer of the news himself. The atmosphere became so threatening, in fact, that it looked as though the executive might have to call security to usher him safely from the room.

The next day, another executive visited the same staff. He

took a very different approach. He spoke from his heart about the crucial importance of journalism to the vibrancy of a society, and of the calling that had drawn them all to the field in the first place. He reminded them that no one goes into journalism to get rich – as a profession its finances have always been marginal, with job security ebbing and flowing with larger economic tides. And he invoked the passion, even the dedication, the journalists had for the service they offered. Finally, he wished them all well in getting on with their careers.

When this leader finished speaking, the staff cheered.

The difference between the leaders lay in the mood and tone with which they delivered their messages: One drove the group toward antagonism and hostility, the other toward optimism, even inspiration, in the face of difficulty. These two moments point to a hidden, but crucial, dimension in leadership – the emotional impact of what a leader says and does.

While most people recognize that a leader's mood – and how he or she impacts the mood of others – plays a significant role in any organization, emotions are often seen as too personal or unquantifiable to talk about in a meaningful way. But research in the field of emotion has yielded keen insights into not only how to measure the impact of a leader's emotions but also how the best leaders have found effective ways to understand and improve the way they handle their own and other people's emotions. Understanding the powerful role of emotions in the workplace sets the best leaders apart from the rest – not just in tangibles such as better business results and the retention of talent, but also in the all-important intangibles, such as higher morale, motivation, and commitment.

THE PRIMAL DIMENSION

This emotional task of the leader is primal – that is, first – in two senses: It is both the original and the most important act of leadership. Leaders have always played a primordial emotional role. No doubt humankind's original leaders – whether tribal chieftains or shamanesses – earned their place in large part because their leadership was emotionally compelling. Throughout history and in cultures everywhere, the leader in any human group has been the one to whom others look for assurance and clarity when facing uncertainty or threat, or when there's a job to be done. The leader acts as the group's emotional guide.

In the modern organization, this primordial emotional task – though by now largely invisible – remains foremost among the many jobs of leadership: driving the collective emotions in a positive direction and clearing the smog created by toxic emotions. This task applies to leadership everywhere, from the boardroom to the shop floor.

Quite simply, in any human group the leader has maximal power to sway everyone's emotions. If people's emotions are pushed toward the range of enthusiasm, performance can soar; if people are driven toward rancor and anxiety, they will be thrown off stride. This indicates another important aspect of primal leadership: Its effects extend beyond ensuring that a job is well done. Followers also look to a leader for supportive emotional connection – for empathy. All leadership includes this primal dimension, for better or for worse. When leaders drive emotions positively, as was the case with the second executive at the BBC, they bring out everyone's best. We call this effect resonance. When they drive emotions negatively, as with the first executive, leaders spawn dissonance, undermining the emotional foundations that let people shine. Whether an organization withers or flourishes depends to a remarkable extent on the leaders' effectiveness in this primal emotional dimension.

The key, of course, to making primal leadership work to everyone's advantage lies in the leadership competencies of emotional intelligence: how leaders handle themselves and their relationships. Leaders who maximize the benefits of primal leadership drive the emotions of those they lead in the right direction.

How does all of this work? Studies of the brain reveal the

neurological mechanisms of primal leadership and make clear just why emotional intelligence abilities are so crucial.

THE OPEN LOOP

The reason a leader's manner – not just what he does, but how he does it – matters so much lies in the design of the human brain: what scientists have begun to call the open loop nature of the limbic system, our emotional centers. A closed-loop system such as the circulatory system is self-regulating; what's happening in the circulatory system of others around us does not impact our own system. An open-loop system depends largely on external sources to manage itself.

In other words, we rely on connections with other people for our own emotional stability. The open-loop limbic system was a winning design in evolution, no doubt, because it allows people to come to one another's emotional rescue – enabling, for example, a mother to soothe her crying infant, or a lookout in a primate band to signal an instant alarm when he perceives a threat.

Despite the veneer of our advanced civilization, the open-loop principle still holds. Research in intensive care units has shown that the comforting presence of another person not only lowers the patient's blood pressure, but also slows the secretion of fatty acids that block arteries.[11] More dramatically, whereas three or more incidents of intense stress within a year (say, serious financial trouble, being fired, or a divorce) triple the death rate in socially isolated middle-aged men, they have no impact whatsoever on the death rate of men who cultivate many close relationships.[12]

Scientists describe the open loop as "interpersonal limbic regulation," whereby one person transmits signals that can alter hormone levels, cardiovascular function, sleep rhythms, and even immune function inside the body of another.[13]

That's how couples who are in love are able to trigger in one another's brains surges of oxytocin, which creates a pleasant, affectionate feeling. But in all aspects of social life, not just love relationships, our physiologies intermingle, our emotions automatically shifting into the register of the person we're with. The open-loop design of the limbic system means that other people can change our very physiology – and so our emotions.

Even though the open-loop is so much a part of our lives, we usually don't notice the process itself. Scientists have captured this attunement of emotions in the laboratory by measuring the physiology – such as heart rate – of two people as they have a good conversation. As the conversation begins, their bodies each operate at different rhythms. But by the end of a simple fifteen-minute conversation, their physiological profiles look remarkably similar – a phenomenon called mirroring. This entrainment occurs strongly during the downward spiral of a conflict, when anger and hurt reverberate, but also goes on more subtly during pleasant interactions.[14] It happens hardly at all during an emotionally neutral discussion. Researchers have seen again and again how emotions spread irresistibly in this way whenever people are near one another, even when the contact is completely nonverbal. For example, when three strangers sit facing each other in silence for a minute or two, the one who is most emotionally expressive transmits his or her mood to the other two – without speaking a single word.[15] The same effect holds in the office, boardroom, or shop floor; people in groups at work inevitably "catch" feelings from one another, sharing everything from jealousy and envy to angst or euphoria. The more cohesive the group, the stronger the sharing of moods, emotional history, and even hot buttons.[16]

In seventy work teams across diverse industries, for instance, members who sat in meetings together ended up sharing moods – either good or bad – within two hours.[17] Nurses, and even accountants, who monitored their moods over weeks or every few hours as they worked together showed emotions that tracked together – and the group's shared moods were largely independent of the hassles they shared.[18] Studies of professional sports teams reveal similar results: Quite apart from the ups and downs of a team's standing, its players tend to synchronize their moods over a period of days and weeks.[19]

CONTAGION AND LEADERSHIP

The continual interplay of limbic open loops among members of a group creates a kind of emotional soup, with everyone adding his or her own flavor to the mix. But it is the leader who adds the strongest seasoning. Why? Because of that enduring reality of business: Everyone watches the boss. People take their emotional cues from the top. Even when the boss isn't highly visible – for example, the CEO who works behind closed doors on an upper floor – his attitude affects the moods of his direct reports, and a domino effect ripples throughout the company's emotional climate.[20]

Careful observations of working groups in action revealed several ways the leader plays such a pivotal role in determining the shared emotions.[21] Leaders typically talked more than anyone else, and what they said was listened to more carefully. Leaders were also usually the first to speak out on a subject, and when others made comments, their remarks most often referred to what the leader had said than to anyone else's comments. Because the leader's way of seeing things has special weight, leaders "manage meaning" for a group, offering a way to interpret, and so react emotionally to, a given situation.[22]

But the impact on emotions goes beyond what a leader says. In these studies, even when leaders were not talking, they were watched more carefully than anyone else in the group. When people raised a question for the group as a whole, they would keep their eyes on the leader to see his or her response. Indeed, group members generally see the leader's emotional reaction as the most valid response, and so model their own on it – particularly in an ambiguous situation, where various members react differently. In a sense, the leader sets the emotional standard.

Leaders give praise or withhold it, criticize well or

destructively, offer support or turn a blind eye to people's needs. They can frame the group's mission in ways that give more meaning to each person's contribution – or not. They can guide in ways that give people a sense of clarity and direction in their work and that encourage flexibility, setting people free to use their best sense of how to get the job done. All these acts help determine a leader's primal emotional impact.

Still, not all "official" leaders in a group are necessarily the emotional leaders. When the designated leader lacks credibility for some reason, people may turn for emotional guidance to someone else who they trust and respect. This de facto leader then becomes the one who molds others' emotional reactions. For instance, a well-known jazz group that was named for its formal leader and founder actually took its emotional cues from a different musician. The founder continued to manage bookings and logistics, but when it came time to decide what tune the group would play next or how the sound system should be adjusted, all eyes turned to the dominant member – the emotional leader.[23]

Regardless of who the emotional leader might be, however, she's likely to have a knack for acting as a limbic "attractor," exerting a palpable force on the emotional brains of people around her. Watch a gifted actor at work, for example, and observe how easily she draws an audience into her emotional orbit. Whether she's conveying the agony of a betrayal or a joyous triumph, the audience feels those things too.

LAUGHTER AND THE OPEN LOOP

Emotions may spread like viruses, but not all emotions spread with the same ease. A study at the Yale University School of Management found that among working groups, cheerfulness and warmth spread most easily, while irritability is less contagious and depression spreads hardly at all.[24] This greater diffusion rate for good moods has direct implications for business results. Moods, the Yale study found, influence how effectively people work; upbeat moods boost cooperation, fairness, and business performance.

Laughter, in particular, demonstrates the power of the open loop in operation – and therefore the contagious nature of all emotion. Hearing laughter, we automatically smile or laugh too, creating a spontaneous chain reaction that sweeps through a group. Glee spreads so readily because our brain includes open-loop circuits, designed specifically for detecting smiles and laughter that make us laugh in response. The result is a positive emotional hijack.

Similarly, of all emotional signals, smiles are the most contagious; they have an almost irresistible power to make others smile in return.[25] Smiles may be so potent because of the beneficial role they played in evolution: Smiles and laughter, scientists speculate, evolved as a nonverbal way to cement alliances, signifying that an individual is relaxed and friendly rather than guarded or hostile.

Laughter offers a uniquely trustworthy sign of this friendliness. Unlike other emotional signals – especially a smile, which can be feigned – laughter involves highly complex neural systems that are largely involuntary: It's harder to fake.[26] So whereas a false smile might easily slip through our emotional radar, a forced laugh has a hollow ring.

In a neurological sense, laughing represents the shortest distance between two people because it instantly interlocks limbic systems. This immediate, involuntary reaction, as one researcher puts it, involves "the most direct communication possible between people – brain to brain – with our intellect just going along for the ride, in what might be called a "limbic lock."[27] No surprise, then, that people who relish each other's company laugh easily and often; those who distrust or dislike each other, or who are otherwise at odds, laugh little together, if at all.

In any work setting, therefore, the sound of laughter signals the group's emotional temperature, offering one sure sign that people's hearts as well as their minds are engaged. Moreover, laughter at work has little to do with someone telling a canned joke: In a study of 1,200 episodes of laughter during social interactions, the laugh almost always came as a friendly response to some ordinary remark like "nice meeting you," not to a punchline.[28] A good laugh sends a reassuring message: We're on the same wavelength, we get along. It signals trust, comfort, and a shared sense of the world; as a rhythm in a conversation, laughing signals that all is well for the moment.

How easily we catch leaders' emotional states, then, has to do with how expressively their faces, voices, and gestures convey their feelings. The greater a leader's skill at transmitting emotions, the more forcefully the emotions will spread. Such transmission does not depend on theatrics, of course; since people pay close attention to a leader, even subtle expressions of emotion can have great impact. Even so, the more open leaders are – how well they express their own enthusiasm, for example – the more readily others will feel that same contagious passion.

Leaders with that kind of talent are emotional magnets; people naturally gravitate to them. If you think about the leaders with whom people most want to work in an organization, they probably have this ability to exude upbeat feelings. It's one reason emotionally intelligent leaders attract talented people – for the pleasure of working in their presence. Conversely, leaders who emit the negative register – who are irritable, touchy, domineering, cold – repel people. No one wants to work for a grouch. Research has proven it: Optimistic, enthusiastic leaders more easily retain their people, compared with those bosses who tend toward negative moods.[29]

Let's now take the impact of primal leadership one step further, to examine just how much emotions determine job effectiveness.

HOW MOODS IMPACT RESULTS

Emotions are highly intense, fleeting, and sometimes disruptive to work; moods tend to be less intense, longer-lasting feelings that typically don't interfere with the job at hand. And an emotional episode usually leaves a corresponding lingering mood: a low-key, continual flow of feeling throughout the group.

Although emotions and moods may seem trivial from a business point of view, they have real consequences for getting work done. A leader's mild anxiety can act as a signal that something needs more attention and careful thought. In fact, a sober mood can help immensely when considering a risky situation – and too much optimism can lead to ignoring dangers.[30] A sudden flood of anger can rivet a leader's attention on an urgent problem – such as the revelation that a senior executive has engaged in sexual harassment – redirecting the leader's energies from the normal round of concerns toward finding a solution, such as improving the organization's efforts to eliminate harassment.[31]

While mild anxiety (such as over a looming deadline) can focus attention and energy, prolonged distress can sabotage a leader's relationships and also hamper work performance by diminishing the brain's ability to process information and respond effectively. A good laugh or an upbeat mood, on the other hand, more often enhances the neural abilities crucial for doing good work.

Both good and bad moods tend to perpetuate themselves, in part because they skew perceptions and memories: When people feel upbeat, they see the positive light in a situation and recall the good things about it, and when they feel bad, they focus on the downside.[32] Beyond this perceptual skew, the stew of stress hormones secreted when a person is upset takes hours to become reabsorbed in the body and fade away. That's why a sour relationship with a boss can leave a person a captive of that distress, with a mind preoccupied and a body unable to calm itself: He got me so upset during that meeting I couldn't go to sleep for hours last night. As a result, we naturally prefer being with people who are emotionally positive, in part because they make us feel good.

EMOTIONAL HIJACKING ——————————————

Negative emotions – especially chronic anger, anxiety, or a sense of futility – powerfully disrupt work, hijacking attention from the task at hand. For instance, in a Yale study of moods and their contagion, the performance of groups making executive decisions about how best to allocate yearly bonuses was measurably boosted by positive feelings and was impaired by negative ones. Significantly, the group members themselves did not realize the influence of their own moods.[33]

Of all the interactions at an international hotel chain that pitched employees into bad moods, the most frequent was talking to someone in management. Interactions with bosses led to bad feelings – frustration, disappointment, anger, sadness, disgust, or hurt – about nine out of ten times. These interactions were the cause of distress more often than customers, work pressure, company policies, or personal problems.[34] Not that leaders need to be overly "nice"; the emotional art of leadership includes pressing the reality of work demands without unduly upsetting people. One of the oldest laws in psychology holds that beyond a moderate level, increases in anxiety and worry erode mental abilities. Distress not only erodes mental abilities, but also makes people less emotionally intelligent. People who are upset have trouble reading emotions accurately in other people – decreasing the most basic skill needed for empathy and, as a result, impairing their social skills.[35]

Another consideration is that the emotions people feel while they work, according to new findings on job satisfaction, reflect most directly the true quality of work life.[36] The percentage of time people feel positive emotions at work turns out to be one of the strongest predictors of satisfaction, and therefore, for instance, of how likely employees are to quit.[37] In this sense, leaders who spread bad moods are simply bad for business – and those who pass along good moods help drive a business's success.

GOOD MOODS, GOOD WORK ————————————

When people feel good, they work at their best. Feeling good lubricates mental efficiency, making people better at understanding information and using decision rules in complex judgments, as well as more flexible in their thinking.[38] Upbeat moods, research verifies, make people view others – or events – in a more positive light. That in turn helps people feel more optimistic about their ability to achieve a goal, enhances creativity and decision-making skills, and predisposes people to be helpful.[39] Insurance agents with a glass-is-half-full outlook, for instance, are far more able than their more pessimistic peers to persist despite rejections, and so they make more sales.[40] Moreover, research on humor at work reveals that a well-timed joke or playful laughter can stimulate creativity, open lines of communication, enhance a sense of connection and trust, and, of course, make work more fun.[41] Playful joking increases the likelihood of financial concessions during a negotiation. Small wonder that playfulness holds a prominent place in the tool kit of emotionally intelligent leaders.

Good moods prove especially important when it comes to teams: The ability of a leader to pitch a group into an enthusiastic, cooperative mood can determine its success. On the other hand, whenever emotional conflicts in a group bleed attention and energy from their shared tasks, a group's performance will suffer.

Consider the results of a study of sixty-two CEOs and their top management teams.[42] The CEOs represented some of the Fortune 500, as well as leading U.S. service companies (such as consulting and accounting firms), not-for-profit organizations, and government agencies. The CEOs and their management team members were assessed on how upbeat – energetic, enthusiastic, determined – they were. They were also asked how much conflict and tumult the top team experienced, that is, personality clashes, anger and friction in meetings, and emotional conflicts (in contrast to disagreement about ideas).

The study found that the more positive the overall moods of people in the top management team, the more cooperatively they worked together – and the better the company's business results. Put differently, the longer a company was run by a management team that did not get along, the poorer that company's market return.

The group IQ, then – the sum total of every person's best talents contributed at full force – depends on the group's emotional intelligence, as shown in its harmony. A leader skilled in collaboration can keep cooperation high and thus ensure that the group's decisions will be worth the effort of meeting. Such leaders know how to balance the group's focus on the task at hand with its attention to the quality of members' relationships. They naturally create a friendly but effective climate that lifts everyone's spirits.

QUANTIFYING THE "FEEL" OF A COMPANY

Common wisdom, of course, holds that employees who feel upbeat will likely go the extra mile to please customers and therefore improve the bottom line. But there's actually a logarithm that predicts that relationship: For every 1 percent improvement in the service climate, there's a 2 percent increase in revenue.[43]

Benjamin Schneider, a professor at the University of Maryland, found in operations as diverse as bank branches, insurance company regional offices, credit card call centers, and hospitals that employees' ratings of service climate predicted customer satisfaction, which drove business results. Likewise, poor morale among frontline customer service reps at a given point in time predicts high turnover – and declining customer satisfaction – up to three years later. This low customer satisfaction, in turn, drives declining revenues.[44]

Of all the aspects of business, superior customer care – that holy grail of any service industry – is perhaps affected most by mood contagion, and therefore by the open-loop aspect of the brain. Customer service jobs are notoriously stressful, with high emotions flowing freely, not just from customers to the front lines but also from workers to customers. From a business viewpoint, of course, bad moods in people who serve customers are bad news. First, rudeness is contagious, creating dissatisfied, even angry, customers – quite apart from whether or not a particular service matter was handled well. Second, grumpy workers serve customers poorly, with sometimes devastating results: Cardiac care units where the nurses' general mood was "depressed" had a death rate among patients four times higher than on comparable units.[45]

By contrast, upbeat moods at the front lines benefit a business. If customers find interactions with a counterperson enjoyable, they start to think of the store as a "nice place" to shop. That means not only more repeat visits, but also good word-of-mouth advertising. Moreover, when service people feel upbeat, they do more to please customers: In a study of thirty–two stores in a U.S. retail chain, outlets with positive salespeople showed the best sales results.[46]

But just what does that finding have to do with leadership? In all of those retail outlets, it was the store manager who created the emotional climate that drove salespeople's moods – and ultimately, sales – in the right direction. When the managers themselves were peppy, confident, and optimistic, their moods rubbed off on the staff. Besides the obvious relationships between climate and working conditions or salary, resonant leaders play a key role. In general, the more emotionally demanding the work, the more empathic and supportive the leader needs to be. Leaders drive the service climate and thus the predisposition of employees to satisfy customers. At an insurance company, for instance, effective leadership influenced service climate among agents to account for a 3 to 4 percent difference in insurance renewals – a seemingly small margin that made a big difference to the business.

Organizational consultants have long assumed a positive link of some kind between a business unit's human climate and its performance. But data connecting the two have been sparse – and so, in practice, leaders could more easily ignore their personal style and its effects on the people they led, focusing instead on "harder" business objectives. But now we have results from a range of industries that link leadership to climate and to business performance, making it possible to quantify the hard difference for business performance made by something as soft as the "feel" of a company.

For instance, at a global food and beverage company, positive climate readings predicted higher yearly earnings at major divisions. And in a study of nineteen insurance companies, the climate created by the CEOs among their direct reports predicted the business performance of the entire organization: In 75 percent of cases, climate alone accurately sorted companies into high versus low profits and growth.[47]

Climate in itself does not determine performance. The factors deciding which companies prove most fit in any given quarter are notoriously complex. But our analyses suggest that, overall, the climate – how people feel about working at a company – can account for 20 to 30 percent of business performance. Getting the best out of people pays off in hard results.

If climate drives business results, what drives climate? Roughly 50 to 70 percent of how employees perceive their organization's climate can be traced to the actions of one person: the leader. More than anyone else, the boss creates the conditions that directly determine people's ability to work well.[48]

In short, leaders' emotional states and actions do affect how the people they lead will feel and therefore perform. How well leaders manage their moods and affect everyone else's moods, then, becomes not just a private matter, but a factor in how well a business will do.

THE SOCIAL BRAIN

Adapted from The Brain and Emotional Intelligence:
New Insights

We are constantly impacting the brain states in other people. In my EI model, "Managing relationships" means, at this level, that we're responsible for how we shape the feelings of those we interact with – for better or for worse. In this sense, relationship skills have to do with managing brain states in other people.

This raises a question. Who sends the emotions that pass between people, and who receives them? One answer, for groups of peers, is that the sender tends to be the most emotionally expressive person in the group. But in groups where there are power differences – in the classroom, at work, in organizations generally – it is the most powerful person who is the emotional sender, setting the emotional state for the rest of the group.

In any human group, people pay most attention to – and put most importance on – what the most powerful person in that group says or does. There are many studies that show, for example, that if the leader of a team is in a positive mood, that spreads an upbeat mood to the others and that collective positivity enhances the group's performance. If the leader projects a negative mood, that spreads in the same way, and the group's performance suffers. This has been found for groups making business decisions, seeking creative solutions – even erecting a tent together.

Such emotional contagion happens whenever people interact, whether in a pair, a group, or an organization. It's most obvious at a sporting event or theatrical performance, where the entire crowd goes through the identical emotion at the same time. This contagion can happen because of our social brain, through circuitry like the mirror neuron system. Person-to-person emotional contagion operates automatically, instantly, unconsciously and out of our intentional control.

There was a study done at Massachusetts General Hospital of doctors and patients during a psychotherapy session. The interaction was videotaped and their physiology was monitored. Afterwards, the patients reviewed the tape, identifying moments when they felt the doctor empathized with them – when they felt heard and understood, in rapport with the doctor, versus feeling really disconnected, thinking: "My doctor doesn't get me, doesn't care about me". In those moments where patients felt disconnected, there was no connection in their physiology, either. But at those moments when the patient said, "Yes, I felt a real connection with the doctor," their physiologies moved in tandem, like a dance. There was also a physiological entrainment, with the doctor and patient's heart rates moving in tandem.

That study reflects the physiology of rapport. There are three ingredients to rapport. The first is paying full attention. Both people need to tune in fully to the other, putting aside distractions. The second is being in synch non–verbally. If two people are really connecting well, and you were to observe that interaction without paying attention to what they were saying (like watching a film with no soundtrack), you'll see their moves are almost choreographed, like a dance. Such synchrony is orchestrated by another set of neurons, called oscillators, which regulate how our body moves in relationship to another body (or any object).

The third ingredient of rapport is positive feeling. It's a kind of micro–flow, an interpersonal high. These moments of interpersonal chemistry, or simpatico, are when things happen at their best – no matter the specifics of what we're doing together.

An article in the Harvard Business Review calls this kind of interaction a "human moment." How do you have a human moment at work? You have to put aside whatever else you're doing, and pay full attention to the person who's with you. And that opens the way to rapport, where emotional flow is in tandem. When your physiology is in synchrony with someone else you feel connected, close and warm. You can read this human moment in terms of physiology – but you can also read it experientially, because during those moments of chemistry we feel good about being with the other person. And that person is feeling good about being with us.

THE SWEET SPOT FOR ACHIEVEMENT

Adapted From Social Intelligence

You are driving to work, planning an important meeting with a colleague, and intermittently reminding yourself that you must remember to turn left at the traffic light, not right as usual, so you can drop your suit at the cleaners.

Suddenly an ambulance screams up behind you, and you speed up to get out of the way. You feel your heart quicken. You try to resume planning the morning's meeting, but your thoughts are disorganized now and you lose concentration, distracted. When you get to work, you berate yourself because you forgot to go to the cleaners.

This scenario comes not from some business primer but from the academic journal Science, as the beginning of an article called "The Biology of Being Frazzled."[49] The article summarizes the effects on thinking and performance caused by being mildly upset – frazzled from the hassles of daily life.

"Frazzle" is a neural state in which emotional upsurges hamper the workings of the executive center. While we are frazzled, we cannot concentrate or think clearly. That neural truth has direct implications for achieving the optimal emotional atmosphere both in the classroom and the office.

From the vantage point of the brain, doing well in school and at work involves one and the same state, the brain's sweet spot for performance. The biology of anxiety casts us out of that zone for excellence.

"Banish fear" was a slogan of the late quality-control

guru W. Edwards Deming. He saw that fear froze a workplace: workers were reluctant to speak up, to share new ideas, or to coordinate well, let alone to improve the quality of their output. The same slogan applies to the classroom – fear frazzles the mind, disrupting learning.

The basic neurobiology of frazzle reflects the body's default plan for emergency. When we are under stress, the HPA axis roars into action, preparing the body for crisis. Among other biological maneuvers, the amygdala commandeers the prefrontal cortex, the brain's executive center. This shift in control to the low road – the brain's subcortical areas – favors automatic habits, as the amygdala draws on knee-jerk responses to save us. The thinking brain gets sidelined for the duration; the high road, the cortex or thinking center, moves too slowly.

As our brain hands decision-making over to the amygdala circuitry, we lose our ability to think at our best. The more intense the pressure, the more our performance and thinking will suffer.[50] The ascendant amygdala handicaps our abilities for learning, for holding information in working memory, for reacting flexibly and creatively, for focusing attention at will, and for planning and organizing effectively. We plunge into what neuroscientists call "cognitive dysfunction."[51]

"The worst period I ever went through at work," a friend confides, "was when the company was restructuring and people were being 'disappeared' daily, followed by lying memos that they were leaving 'for personal reasons.' No one could focus while that fear was in the air. No real work got done."

Small wonder. The greater the anxiety we feel, the more impaired is the brain's cognitive efficiency. In this zone of mental misery, distracting thoughts hijack our attention and squeeze our cognitive resources. Because high anxiety shrinks the space available to our attention, it undermines our very capacity to take in new information, let alone generate fresh ideas. Near-panic is the enemy of learning and creativity.

The neural highway for dysphoria runs from the amygdala to the right side of the prefrontal cortex. As this circuitry activates, our thoughts fixate on what has triggered the distress. And as we become preoccupied by, say, worry or resentment, our mental agility sputters. Likewise, when we are sad, activity levels in the prefrontal cortex drop and we generate fewer thoughts.[52] Extremes of anxiety and anger on the one hand, and sadness on the other, push brain activity beyond its zones for effectiveness. Boredom fogs the brain with its own brand of inefficiency. As minds wander, they lose focus; motivation vanishes. In any meeting that has gone on too long (as so many do), the vacant eyes of those trapped at the table will betray this inner absence. And we all remember days of ennui as students, absently staring out the window.

But joyous moments, says University of Southern California neuroscientist Antonio Damasio, signify "optimal physiological coordination and smooth running of the operations of life." Damasio, one of the world's leading neuroscientists, has long been a pioneer in linking findings in brain science to human experience. Damasio argues that more than merely letting us survive the daily grind, joyous states allow us to flourish, to live well, and to feel well-being.

Such upbeat states, he notes, allow a "greater ease in the capacity to act," a greater harmony in our functioning that enhances our power and freedom in whatever we do. The field of cognitive science, Damasio notes, in studying the neural networks that run mental operations, finds similar conditions and dubs them "maximal harmonious states."

When the mind runs with such internal harmony, ease, efficiency, rapidity, and power are at a maximum. We experience such moments with a quiet thrill. Imaging studies show that while people are in such exhilarating, up-beat states, the area of the brain that displays most activity is in the prefrontal cortex, the hub of the high road.

Heightened prefrontal activity enhances mental abilities like creative thinking, cognitive flexibility, and the processing of information.[53] Even physicians, paragons of rationality, think

88

more clearly when in good moods. Radiologists work with greater speed and accuracy after getting a small mood-boosting gift – and their diagnostic notes include more helpful suggestions for further treatment, as well as more offers to do further consultation.[54]

AN UPSIDE-DOWN U

Plotting the relationship between mental adeptness (and performance generally) and the spectrum of moods creates what looks like an upside-down U with its legs spread out a bit. Joy, cognitive efficiency, and outstanding performance occur at the peak of the inverted U. Along the downside of one leg lies boredom, along the other anxiety. The more apathy or angst we feel, the worse we do, whether on a term paper or an office memo.

We are lifted out of the daze of boredom as a challenge piques our interest, our motivation increases, and attention focuses. The height of cognitive performance occurs where motivation and focus peak, at the intersection of a task's difficulty and our ability to match its demand. At a tipping point just past this peak of cognitive efficiency, challenges begin to exceed ability, and so the downside of the inverted U begins.

We taste panic as we realize, say, we've procrastinated disastrously long on that paper or memo. From there our increasing anxiety erodes our cognitive efficiency.[55] As tasks multiply in difficulty and challenge melts into overwhelm, the low road becomes increasingly active. The executive center frazzles as the challenges engulf our abilities, and the brain hands the reins to the emotional centers. This neural shift of control accounts for the shape of the upside-down U.

Stress Hormones and Performance

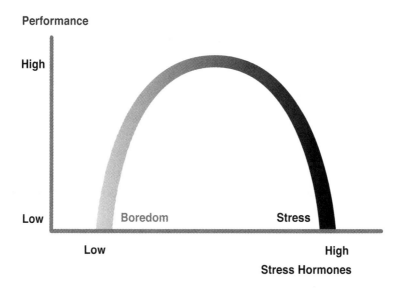

An upside-down U graphs the relationship between levels of stress and mental performance such as learning or decision-making. Stress varies with challenge; at the low end, too little breeds disinterest and boredom, while as challenge increases it boosts interest, attention, and motivation – which at their optimal level produce maximum cognitive efficiency and achievement. As challenges continue to rise beyond our skill to handle them, stress intensifies; at its extreme, our performance and learning collapse.

The inverted U reflects the impact of two different neural systems on learning and performance. Both build as enhanced attention and motivation increase the activity of the glucocorticoid system; healthy levels of cortisol energize us for engagement.[56] Positive moods elicit the mild-to-moderate range of cortisol associated with better learning.

But if stress continues to climb after that optimal point where people learn and perform at their best, a second neural system kicks in to secrete norepinephrine at the high levels found when we feel outright fear.[57] From this point – the start of that downward slope toward panic – the more stress escalates, the worse our mental efficiency and performance become. During high anxiety the brain secretes high levels of cortisol plus norepinephrine that interfere with the smooth operation of neural mechanisms for learning and memory. When these stress hormones reach a critical level, they enhance amygdala function but debilitate the prefrontal areas, which lose their ability to contain amygdala-driven impulses.

As any student knows who has suddenly found himself studying harder as a test approaches, a modicum of pressure enhances motivation and focuses attention. Up to a point, selective attention increases as levels of pressure ratchet upward, like looming deadlines, a teacher watching, or a challenging assignment. Paying fuller attention means that working memory operates with more cognitive efficiency, culminating in maximum mental ease. But at a tipping point just past the optimal state – where challenges begin to overmatch ability – increasing anxiety starts to erode cognitive efficiency. For example, in this zone of performance disaster, students with math anxiety have less attention available when they tackle a math problem. Their anxious worrying occupies the attentional space they need, impairing their ability to solve problems or grasp new concepts.

All of this directly affects how well we do in the classroom – or on the job. While we are distressed, we don't think clearly, and we tend to lose interest in pursuing even goals that are important to us. Psychologists who have studied the effects of mood on learning conclude that when students are neither attentive nor happy in class, they absorb only a fraction of the information being presented.[58]

The drawbacks apply as well to leaders. Foul feelings weaken empathy and concern. For example, managers in bad moods give more negative performance appraisals, focusing only on the downside, and are more disapproving in their opinions.[59] We do best at moderate to challenging levels of stress; while the mind frazzles under extreme pressure.

POWER AND EMOTIONAL FLOW

Whenever a meeting threatened to lapse into malaise, the president of a company would suddenly launch into a critique of someone at the table who could take it (usually the marketing director, who was his best friend). Then he would swiftly move on, having riveted the attention of everyone in the room. That tactic invariably revived the group's failing focus with keen interest. He was herding those in attendance up the inverted U from boredom to engagement.

Displays of a leader's displeasure make use of emotional contagion. If artfully calibrated, even a burst of pique can stir followers enough to capture their attention and motivate them. Many effective leaders sense that – like compliments – well-titrated doses of irritation can energize. The measure of how well calibrated a message of displeasure might be is whether it moves people toward their performance peak or plummets them past the tipping point into the zone where distress corrodes performance.

Not all emotional partners are equal. A power dynamic operates in emotional contagion, determining which person's brain will more forcefully draw the other into its emotional orbit. Mirror neurons are leadership tools: Emotions flow with special strength from the more socially dominant person to the less.

As aforementioned, people in any group naturally pay more attention to and place more significance on what the most powerful person in that group says and does. That amplifies the force of whatever emotional message the leader may be sending, making her emotions particularly contagious. As I heard the head of a small organization say rather ruefully, "When my mind is full of anger, other people catch it like the flu."

This emotional potency was tested when fifty-six heads of simulated work teams were themselves moved into a good or bad mood, and their subsequent emotional impact on the groups they led was assessed.[60] Team members with upbeat leaders reported that they were feeling in better moods. Perhaps more to the point, they coordinated their work better, getting more done with less effort. On the other hand, the teams with grumpy bosses were thrown out of synch, making them inefficient. Worse, their panicked efforts to please the leader led to bad decisions and poorly chosen strategies.

While a boss's artfully couched displeasure can be an effective goad, fuming is self-defeating as a leadership tactic. When leaders habitually use displays of bad moods to motivate, more work may seem to get done – but it will not necessarily be better work. And relentlessly foul moods corrode the emotional climate, sabotaging the brain's ability to work at its best.

In this sense, leadership boils down to a series of social exchanges in which the leader can drive the other person's emotions into a better or worse state. In high-quality exchanges, the subordinate feels the leader's attention and empathy, support, and positivity. In low-quality interactions, he feels isolated and threatened.

The passing of moods from leader to follower typifies any relationship where one person has power over another, such as teacher-student, doctor-patient, and parent-child. Despite the power differential in these relationships, they all have a benign potential: to promote the growth, education, or healing of the less powerful person.

Another powerful reason for leaders to be mindful of what they say to employees: people recall negative interactions with a boss with more intensity, in more detail, and more often than they do positive ones. The ease with which demotivation can be spread by a boss makes it all the more imperative for him to act in ways that make the emotions left behind uplifting ones.[61]

Callousness from a boss not only heightens the risk of losing good people, it torpedoes cognitive efficiency. A socially intelligent leader helps people contain and recover from their emotional distress. If only from a business perspective, a leader would do well to react with empathy rather than indifference — and to act on it.

BOSSES: THE GOOD, THE BAD, AND THE UGLY

Any collection of working people can readily recall two kinds of bosses they've known, one they loved to work for, and one they couldn't wait to escape. I've asked for such a list from dozens of groups, ranging from meetings of CEOs to conventions of school teachers, in cities as different as Sao Paulo, Brussels, and St. Louis. The lists that disparate groups generate, no matter where they are, are remarkably similar to this one:

GOOD BOSS	BAD BOSS
GREAT LISTENER	BLANK WALL
ENCOURAGER	DOUBTER
COMMUNICATOR	SECRETIVE
COURAGEOUS	INTIMIDATING
SENSE OF HUMOR	BAD TEMPER
SHOWS EMPATHY	SELF-CENTERED
DECISIVE	INDECISIVE
TAKES RESPONSIBILITY	BLAMES
HUMBLE	ARROGANT
SHARES AUTHORITY	MISTRUSTS

The best bosses are people who are trustworthy, empathic and connected, who make us feel calm, appreciated, and inspired. The worst – distant, difficult, and arrogant – make us feel uneasy at best and resentful at worst.

Those contrasting sets of attributes map well on the kind of parent who fosters security on the one hand, and anxiety on the other. In fact, the emotional dynamic at work in managing employees shares much with parenting. Our parents form our basic template for a secure base in childhood, but others continue to add to it as we go through life. In school, our teachers fill that position; at work, our boss.

"Secure bases are sources of protection, energy and comfort, allowing us to free our own energy," George Kohlrieser told me. Kohlrieser, a psychologist and professor of leadership at the International Institute for Management Development in Switzerland, observes that having a secure base at work is crucial for high performance.

Feeling secure, Kohlrieser argues, lets a person focus better on the work at hand, achieve goals, and see obstacles as challenges, not threats. Those who are anxious, in contrast, readily become preoccupied with the specter of failure, fearing that doing poorly will mean they will be rejected or abandoned (in this context, fired) – and so they play it safe.

People who feel that their boss provides a secure base, Kohlrieser finds, are more free to explore, be playful, take risks, innovate, and take on new challenges. Another business benefit: if leaders establish such trust and safety, then when they give tough feedback, the person receiving it not only stays more open but sees benefit in getting even hard-to-take information.

Like a parent, however, a leader should not protect employees from every tension or stress; resilience grows from a modicum of discomfort generated by necessary pressures at work. But since too much stress overwhelms, an astute leader acts as a secure base by lessening overwhelming pressures if possible – or at least not making them worse.

For instance, a midlevel executive tells me, "My boss is a

superb buffer. Whatever financial performance pressures he gets from headquarters – and they are considerable – he does not pass them down to us. The head of a sister division in our corporation, though, does, subjecting all his employees to a personal profit-and-loss evaluation every quarter – even though the products they develop take two to three years to come to market."

On the other hand, if members of a work team are resilient, highly motivated, and good at what they do – in other words, if they have high tipping points on the inverted U – a leader can be challenging and demanding and still get good results. Yet disaster can result when such a high-pressure leader shifts to a less gung-ho culture. An investment banker tells me of a "hard driving, bottom line, 24/7" leader who yelled when displeased. When he merged his company with another, "the same style that worked for him before drove away all the managers in the acquired business, who saw him as intolerable. The company's stock price still had not risen two years after the merger."

No child can avoid emotional pain while growing up, and likewise emotional toxicity seems to be a normal by-product of organizational life-people are fired, unfair policies come from headquarters, frustrated employees turn in anger on others. The causes are legion: abusive bosses or unpleasant coworkers, frustrating procedures, chaotic change. Reactions range from anguish and rage, to lost confidence or hopelessness.

Perhaps luckily, we do not have to depend only on the boss. Colleagues, a work team, friends at work, and even the organization itself can create the sense of having a secure base. Everyone in a given workplace contributes to the emotional stew, the sum total of the moods that emerge as they interact through the workday. No matter what our designated role may be, how we do our work, interact, and make each other feel adds to the overall emotional tone.

Whether it's a supervisor or fellow worker who we can turn to when upset, their mere existence has a tonic benefit. For many working people, coworkers become something like a "family," a group in which members feel a strong emotional attachment for one another. This makes them especially loyal to each other as a team. The stronger the emotional bonds among workers, the more motivated, productive, and satisfied with their work they are.

Our sense of engagement and satisfaction at work results in large part from the hundreds and hundreds of daily interactions we have while there, whether with a supervisor, colleagues, or customers. The accumulation and frequency of positive versus negative moments largely determines our satisfaction and ability to perform; small exchanges–a compliment on work well done, a word of support after a setback–add up to how we feel on the job.[62]

Even having just one person who can be counted on at work can make a telling difference in how we feel. In surveys of more than five million people working in close to five hundred organizations, one of the best predictors of how happy someone felt on their job was agreement with the statement, "I have a best friend at work."[63]

The more such sources of emotional support we have in our worklife, the better off we are. A cohesive group with a secure – and security-promoting – leader creates an emotional surround that can be so contagious that even people who tend to be highly anxious find themselves relaxing.

As the head of a high-performing scientific team told me, "I never hire anyone for my lab without them working with us provisionally for a while. Then I ask the other people in the lab their opinions, and I defer to them. If the interpersonal chemistry is not good, I don't want to risk hiring someone – no matter how good they may be otherwise."

THE SOCIALLY INTELLIGENT LEADER

The human resources department of a large corporation arranged a daylong workshop by a famous expert in the company's area of specialty. A larger-than-expected crowd showed up, and at the last minute the event was switched to a larger room, one that could hold everyone but was poorly equipped. As a result, the people in the back had trouble seeing or hearing the speaker. At the morning break, a woman sitting in the back marched up to the head of human resources shaking with rage and complaining that she could neither glimpse the screen on which the speaker's image was being projected, nor make out his words.

"I knew that all I could do was listen, empathize, acknowledge her problem, and tell her I'd do my best to fix things," the head of human resources told me. "At the break she saw me go to the audiovisual people and at least try to get the screen higher. I couldn't do much at all about the bad acoustics.

"I saw that woman again at the end of the day. She told me she couldn't really hear or see all that much better, but now she was relaxed about it. She really appreciated my hearing her out and trying to help."

When people in an organization feel angry and distressed, a leader, like that HR head, can at least listen with empathy, show concern, and make a goodwill effort to change things for the better.

Whether or not that effort solves the problem, it does some good emotionally. By attending to someone's feelings, the leader helps metabolize them, so the person can move on rather then continuing to seethe.

The leader need not necessarily agree with the person's position or reaction. But simply acknowledging their point of view, then apologizing if necessary or otherwise seeking a remedy, defuses some of the toxicity, rendering destructive emotions less harmful. In a survey of employees at seven hundred companies, the majority said that a caring boss was more important to them than how much they earned.[64] This finding has business implications beyond just making people feel good. The same survey found that employees' liking for their boss was a prime driver of both productivity and the length of time they stayed at that job. Given the choice, people don't want to work for a toxic boss at nearly any wage – except to get enough "screw you" money to quit with security.

Socially intelligent leadership starts with being fully present and getting in synch. Once a leader is engaged, then the full panoply of social intelligence can came into play, from sensing how people feel and why, to interacting smoothly enough to move people into a positive state. There is no magic recipe for what to do in every situation, no five-steps-to-social-intelligence-at-work. But whatever we do as we interact, the single measure of its success will be where in the inverted U each person ends up.

Businesses are on the front lines of applying social intelligence. As people work longer and longer hours, businesses loom as their substitute family, village, and social network – yet most of us can be tossed out at the will of management. That inherent ambivalence means that in more and more organizations, hope and fear run rampant.

Excellence in people management cannot ignore these subterranean affective currents: they have real human consequences, and they matter for people's abilities to perform at their best. And because emotions are so contagious, every boss at every level needs to remember he or she can make matters either worse or better.

— DEVELOPING EMOTIONAL — INTELLIGENCE

Adapted from The Brain and Emotional Intelligence:
New Insights

You may have heard that we're born with a huge amount of brain cells, and then we lose them steadily until we die. Now, the good news: that's neuromythology.

The new understanding is what's called 'neurogenesis': Every day the brain generates 10,000 stem cells that split into two. One becomes a daughter line that continues making stem cells, and the other migrates to wherever it's needed in the brain and becomes that kind of cell. Very often that destination is where the cell is needed for new learning. Over the next four months, that new cell forms about 10,000 connections with others to create new neural circuitry.

The state of the art in mapping this will be coming out of labs like Richard Davidson's that have massive computing power, because new, innovative software tools for brain imaging can now track and show this new connectivity at the single–cell level.

Neurogenesis adds power to our understanding of neuroplasticity, that the brain continually reshapes itself according to the experiences we have. If we are learning a new golf swing, that circuitry will attract connections and neurons. If we are changing a habit – say trying to get better at listening – then that circuitry will grow accordingly.

On the other hand, when we try to overcome a bad habit, we're up against the thickness of the circuitry for something we've practiced and repeated thousands of times. So what are the brain lessons for coaching, or for working on our own to enhance an emotional intelligence skill?

First, get committed. Mobilize the motivating power in the left prefrontal areas. If you're a coach, you've got to engage the person, get them enthused about achieving the goal of change. Here it helps to draw on their dreams, their vision for themselves, where they want to be in the future. Then work from where they are now on what they might improve to help them get where they want to go in life.

If you can, at this point it's helpful to get 360-degree feedback on the emotional intelligence competencies. It's best to use an instrument that measures the emotional intelligence abilities, and lets you ask people whose opinions you value to rate you anonymously on specific behaviors that reflect the competencies of star performers and leaders. Richard Boyatzis and I, working with the Hay Group, have designed a leadership assessment tool, called the Emotional and Social Competence Inventory, or ESCI–360. A trained consultant can help you use this feedback to determine what competencies you would most benefit from strengthening.

The next step is to get very practical: Don't take on trying to learn too much all at once. Operationalize your goal at the level of a specific behavior. Make it practical, so you know exactly what to do and when. For example, say someone has "Blackberry syndrome": a bad habit of multi-tasking and essentially ignoring others, which undermines the full attention that can lead to rapport and good chemistry. You have to break the habit of multi-tasking. So the person might make up an intentional learning plan that says something like: at every naturally occurring opportunity – when a person walks into your office, say, or you come up to a person – you turn off your cell phone and your beeper, turn away from your computer, turn off your daydream or your preoccupation and pay full attention. That gives you a precise piece of behavior to try to change.

So what will help with that? Noticing when a moment like that is about to come, and doing the right thing. Doing the wrong thing is a habit that you have become an Olympic level master at – your neural wiring has made it a default option, what you do automatically. The neural connectivity for that is strong. When you start to form the new, better habit you are essentially creating new circuitry that competes with your old habit in a kind of neural Darwinism. To make the new habit strong enough, you've got to use the power of neuroplasticity – you have to do it over and over again.

If you persist in the better habit, that new circuitry will connect and become more and more powerful, until one day you'll do the right thing in the right way without a second thought. That means the circuitry has become so connected and thick that this is the brain's new default option. With that change in the brain, the better habit will become your automatic choice.

For how long and how many times does an action have to be repeated until it's actually hard-wired? A habit begins to be hard-wired the very first time you practice it. The more you practice it, the more connectivity. How often you have to repeat it so that it becomes the new default of the brain depends in part on how strong the old habit is that it will replace. It usually takes three to six months of using all naturally occurring practice opportunities before the new habit comes more naturally than the old.

Another practice opportunity can occur whenever you have a little free time: mental rehearsal. Mental rehearsal activates the same neural circuitry as does the real activity. This is why Olympic athletes spend the off-season running through their moves in their brain – because that counts as practice time, too. It's going to increase their ability to perform when the real moment comes.

Richard Boyatzis has used this method with his MBA students for years at the Weatherhead School of Management at Case Western Reserve University. And he's followed these students into their jobs as much as seven years later – and found the competecies they had enhanced in his class were still rated as strong by their co-workers.

APPENDIX

Leadership Competencies
Adapted from Primal Leadership

SELF-AWARENESS

• *Emotional self-awareness.* Leaders high in emotional self awareness are attuned to their inner signals, recognizing how their feelings affect them and their job performance. They are attuned to their guiding values and can often intuit the best course of action, seeing the big picture in a complex situation. Emotionally self-aware leaders can be candid and authentic, able to speak openly about their emotions or with conviction about their guiding vision.

• *Accurate self-assessment.* Leaders with high self-awareness typically know their limitations and strengths, and exhibit a sense of humor about themselves. They exhibit a gracefulness in learning where they need to improve, and welcome constructive criticism and feedback. Accurate self-assessment lets a leader know when to ask for help and where to focus in cultivating new leadership strengths.

• *Self-confidence.* Knowing their abilities with accuracy allows leaders to play to their strengths. Self-confident leaders can welcome a difficult assignment. Such leaders often have a sense of presence, a self-assurance that lets them stand out in a group.

SELF-MANAGEMENT

• *Self-control.* Leaders with emotional self-control find ways to manage their disturbing emotions and impulses, and even to channel them in useful ways. A hallmark of self-control is the leader who stays calm and clear-headed under high stress or during a crisis-or who remains unflappable even when confronted by a trying situation.

• **Transparency.** Leaders who are transparent live their values. Transparency - an authentic openness to others about one's feelings, beliefs, and actions - allows integrity. Such leaders openly admit mistakes or faults, and confront unethical behavior in others rather than turn a blind eye.

• **Adaptability.** Leaders who are adaptable can juggle multiple demands without losing their focus or energy, and are comfortable with the inevitable ambiguities of organizational life. Such leaders can be flexible in adapting to new challenges, nimble in adjusting to fluid change, and limber in their thinking in the face of new data or realities.

• **Achievement.** Leaders with strength in achievement have high personal standards that drive them to constantly seek performance improvements-both for themselves and those they lead. They are pragmatic, setting measurable but challenging goals, and are able to calculate risk so that their goals are worthy but attainable. A hallmark of achievement is in continually learning - and teaching ways to do better.

• **Initiative.** Leaders who have a sense of efficacy-that they have what it takes to control their own destiny-excel in initiative. They seize opportunities-or create them rather than simply waiting. Such a leader does not hesitate to cut through red tape, or even bend the rules, when necessary to create better possibilities for the future.

• **Optimism.** A leader who is optimistic can roll with the punches, seeing an opportunity rather than a threat in a setback. Such leaders see others positively, expecting the best of them. And their "glass half-full" outlook leads them to expect that changes in the future will be for the better.

SOCIAL AWARENESS

• *Empathy.* Leaders with empathy are able to attune to a wide range of emotional signals, letting them sense the felt, but unspoken, emotions in a person or group. Such leaders listen attentively and can grasp the other person's perspective. Empathy makes a leader able to get along well with people of diverse backgrounds or from other cultures.

• *Organizational awareness.* A leader with a keen social awareness can be politically astute, able to detect crucial social networks and read key power relationships. Such leaders can understand the political forces at work in an organization, as well as the guiding values and unspoken rules that operate among people there.

• *Service.* Leaders high in the service competence foster an emotional climate so that people directly in touch with the customer or client will keep the relationship on the right track. Such leaders monitor customer or client satisfaction carefully to ensure they are getting what they need. They also make themselves available as needed.

RELATIONSHIP MANAGEMENT

• *Inspiration.* Leaders who inspire both create resonance and move people with a compelling vision or shared mission. Such leaders embody what they ask of others, and are able to articulate a shared mission in a way that inspires others to follow. They offer a sense of common purpose beyond the day-to-day tasks, making work exciting.

• *Influence.* Indicators of a leader's powers of influence range from finding just the right appeal for a given listener to knowing how to build buy-in from key people and a network of support for an initiative. Leaders adept in influence are persuasive and engaging when they address a group.

• **Developing others**. Leaders who are adept at cultivating people's abilities show a genuine interest in those they are helping along, understanding their goals, strengths, and weaknesses. Such leaders can give timely and constructive feedback and are natural mentors or coaches.

• **Change catalyst**. Leaders who can catalyze change are able to recognize the need for the change, challenge the status quo, and champion the new order. They can be strong advocates for the change even in the face of opposition, making the argument for it compellingly. They also find practical ways to overcome barriers to change.

• **Conflict management**. Leaders who manage conflicts best are able to draw out all parties, understand the differing perspectives, and then find a common ideal that everyone can endorse. They surface the conflict, acknowledge the feelings and views of all sides, and then redirect the energy toward a shared ideal.

• **Teamwork and collaboration**. Leaders who are able team players generate an atmosphere of friendly collegiality and are themselves models of respect, helpfulness, and cooperation. They draw others into active, enthusiastic commitment to the collective effort, and build spirit and identity. They spend time forging and cementing close relationships beyond mere work obligations.

ENDNOTES

Taking Stock

1 J. D. Mayer, P. Salovey, and D. R. Caruso, "Models of Emotional Intelligence," in R. J. Sternberg, ed., Handbook of Intelligence, Cambridge, Eng.: Cambridge University Press, 2000.

2 The crash of the intimidating pilot: Carl Lavin, "When Moods Affect Safety: Communications in a Cockpit Mean a Lot a Few Miles Up," The New York Times (June 26, 1994).

3 The survey of 250 executives: Michael Maccoby, "The Corporate Climber Has to Find His Heart," Fortune (Dec. 1976).

4 The story of the sarcastic vice president was told to me by Hendrie Weisinger, a psychologist at the UCLA Graduate School of Business. His book is The Critical Edge: How to Criticize Up and Down the Organization and Make It Pay Off (Boston: Little, Brown, 1989).

5 The survey of times managers blew up was done by Robert Baron, a psychologist at Rensselaer Polytechnic Institute, whom I interviewed for The New York Times (Sept. 11, 1990).

Managing With Heart

6 Criticism as a cause of conflict: Robert Baron, "Countering the Effects of Destructive Criticism: The Relative Efficacy of Four Interventions," journal of Applied Psychology 75, 3 (1990).

7 Specific and vague criticism: Harry Levinson, "Feedback to Subordinates" Addendum to the Levinson Letter, Levinson Institute, Waltham, MA (1992).

8 The concept of group intelligence is set forth in Wendy Williams and Robert Sternberg, "Group Intelligence: Why Some Groups Are Better Than Others" Intelligence (1988).

9 The study of the stars at Bell Labs was reported in Robert Kelley and Janet Caplan, "How Bell Labs Creates Star Performers," Harvard Business Review (July-Aug. 1993).

10 The usefulness of informal networks is noted by David Krackhardt and Jeffrey R. Hanson, "Informal Networks: The Company Behind the Chart," Harvard Business Review (July-Aug. 1993), p. 104

11 The comforting effect: Lisa Berkman et al., "Emotional Support and Survival after Myocardial Infarction," Annals of Internal Medicine (1992).

12 Stress and death: Anika Rosengren et al., "Stressful Life Events, Social Support and Mortality in Men Born in 1933," British Medical Journal 207, no. 17(1983): 1102-1106.

The Group IQ

13 Limbic regulation: Thomas Lewis, Fari Amini, and Richard Lannon, A General Theory of Love (New York: Random House, 2000).

14 Emotional mirroring: Robert Levenson, University of California at Berkeley, personal communication.

15 Expressiveness transmits moods: Howard Friedman and Ronald Riggio, "Effect of Individual Differences in Nonverbal Expressiveness on Transmission of Emotion," Journal of Nonverbal Behavior 6 (1981): 32-58.

16 Groups have moods: Janice R. Kelly and Sigal Barsade, "Moods and Emotions in Small Groups and Work Teams," working paper, Yale School of Management, New Haven, Connecticut, 2001.

Primal Leadership

17 Work teams share moods: C. Bartel and R. Saavedra, "The Collective Construction of Work Group Moods," Administrative Science Quarterly 45 (2000): 187-231.

18 Nurses and accountants tracking moods: Peter Totterdell et al., "Evidence of Mood Linkage in Work Groups," Journal of Personality and Social Psychology 74 (1998): 1504-1515.

19 Sports teams: Peter Totterdell, "Catching Moods and Hitting Runs: Mood Linkage and Subjective Performance in Professional Sports Teams," Journal of Applied Psychology 85, no. 6 (2000): 848-859.

20 The leadership ripple effect: See Wallace Bachman, "Nice Guys Finish First: A SYMLOG Analysis of U.S. Naval Commands," in The SYMLOG Practitioner: Applications of Small Group Research, eds. Richard Brian Polley, A. Paul Hare, and Philip J. Stone (New York: Praeger, 1988).

21 The leader's emotional impact in work groups: Anthony T. Pescosolido, "Emotional Intensity in Groups" (Ph.D. diss., Department of Organizational Behavior, Case Western Reserve University, 2000).

22 Leaders as the managers of meaning: Howard Gardner, Leading Minds: An Anatomy of Leadership (New York: Basic Books, 1995).

23 Informal leaders: V. U. Druskat and A. T. Pascosolido, "Leading Self-Managing Work Teams from the Inside: Informal Leader Behavior and Team Outcomes." Submitted for publication, 2001.

24 Moods, contagion, and work performance: Sigal Barsade and Donald E. Gibson, "Group Emotion: A View from the Top and Bottom," in Research on Managing Groups and Teams, eds. D. Gruenfeld et al. (Greenwich, CT: JAI Press, 1998).

25 Smiles the most contagious: Robert Levenson and Anna Ruef, "Emotional Knowledge and Rapport," in Empathic Accuracy, ed. William Ickes (New York: Guilford Press, 1997).

26 Laughter is involuntary: Meredith Small, "More Than the Best Medicine," Scientific American, August 2000, 24.

27 Laughter is "brain to brain": Robert Provine, Laughter: A Scientific Investigation (New York: Viking Press, 2000), 133.

28 Laughter episodes: Ibid.

29 Good moods in a leader mean lower voluntary turnover: See, for example, Jennifer M. George and Kenneth Bettenhausen, "Understanding Prosocial Behavior, Sales Performance, and Turnover: A Group-Level Analysis in Service Context," Journal of Applied Psychology 75, no. 6 (1990): 698-706.

30 Sober mood and high-risk decisions: R. C. Sinclair, "Mood, Categorization Breadth, and Performance Appraisal," Organizational Behavior and Human Decision Processes 42 (1988): 22-46.

31 Anger and leadership: Jennifer M. George, "Emotions and Leadership: The Role of Emotional Intelligence," Human Relations 53, no. 8 (2000): 1027-1055.

32 Moods perpetuate themselves: A voluminous literature shows the self-reinforcing effect of moods. See, for example, Gordon H. Bower, "Mood Congruity of Social Judgments," in Emotion and Social Judgments, ed. Joseph Forgas (Oxford: Pergamon Press, 1991), 31-53.

33 The Yale study of mood and performance: Sigal Barsade, "The Ripple Effect: Emotional Contagion in Groups," working paper 98, Yale School of

Management, New Haven, Connecticut, 2000.

34 Bosses and bad feelings: John Basch and Cynthia D. Fisher, "Affective Events-Emotions Matrix: A Classification of Job-Related Events and Emotions Experienced in the Workplace," in Emotions in the Workplace: Research, Theory and Practice, ed. N. Ashkanasy, W. Zerbe, and C. Hartel (Westport, CT: Quorum Books, 2000), 36-48.

35 Distress impairs empathy and social skill: Jeffrey B. Henriques and Richard J. Davidson, "Brain Electrical Asymmetries during Cognitive Task Performance in Depressed and Nondepressed Subjects," Biological Psychiatry 42 (1997): 1039-1050.

36 Emotions reflect quality of work life: Cynthia D. Fisher and Christopher S. Noble, "Affect and Performance: A Within Persons Analysis" (paper presented at the Annual Meeting of the Academy of Management, Toronto, 2000).

37 Job satisfaction is not the same as feeling good while working: Cynthia D. Fisher, "Mood and Emotions while Working: Missing Pieces of Job Satisfaction? ," Journal of Organizational Behavior 21 (2000): 185 -202. See also Howard Weiss, Jeffrey Nicholas, and Catherine Daus, "An Examination of the Joint Effects of Affective Experiences and Job Beliefs on Job Satisfaction and Variations in Affective Experiences over Time," Organizational Behavior and Human Decision Processes 78, no. 1 (1999): 1-24.

38 Mental benefits of good moods: See A. M. lsen, "Positive Affect," in Handbook of Cognition and Emotion, eds. Tim Dalgleish and) Mick J. Power (Chichester, England: Wiley, 1999.

39 Good moods and performance: See C. D. Fisher and C. S. Noble, "Emotion and the Illusory Correlation between Job Satisfaction and Job Performance" (paper presented at the second Conference on Emotions in Organizational Life, Toronto, August 2000).

40 Insurance sales: Martin E. Seligman and Peter Schulman, "The People Make the Place," Personnel Psychology 40 (1987): 437-453.

41 The impact of humor on work effectiveness: The findings are reviewed in R. W. Clouse and K. L. Spurgeon, "Corporate Analysis of Humor," Psychology: A Journal of Human Behavior 32 (1995): 1-24.

42 CEOs and their top management team: Sigal G. Barsade, Andrew J. Ward, et al. "To Your Heart's Content: A Mode of Affective Diversity in Top Management Teams," Administrative Science Quarterly 45 (2000): 802-836.

43 Improvement in service climate drives increase in revenue: Lyle Spencer, paper presented at the meeting of the Consortium for Research on Emotional Intelligence in Organizations (Cambridge, Massachusetts, 19 April 2001).

44 Poor customer service rep morale and decline in revenues: Schneider and Bowen, Winning the Service Game.

45 Mood affects cardiac care unit. Benjamin Schneider and D. E. Bowen, Winning the Service Game (Boston: Harvard Business School Press, 1995).

46 Mood, customer service, and sales: George and Bettenhausen, "Understanding Prosocial Behavior."

47 The analysis linking climate to business performance: David McClelland, "Identifying Competencies with Behavioral-Event Interviews," Psychological Science 9 (1998): 331-339; Daniel Williams, "Leadership for the 21st Century: Life Insurance Leadership Study"(Boston: LOMA/Hay Group, 1995).

48 More technically, the styles were found to account for 53 to 72 percent of the variance in organizational climate. See Stephen P. Kelner Jr., Christine A. Rivers, and Kathleen H, O'Connell, "Managerial Style as a Behavioral Predictor of Organizational Climate" (Boston: McBer & Company, 1996).

49 Amy Arnsten, "The Biology of Being Frazzled," Science 280 (1998), pp. 1711-13.

50 On stress intensity and impairment, see J. T. Noteboom et al., "Activation of the Arousal Response and Impairment of Performance Increase with Anxiety and Stressor Intensity," Journal of Applied Physiology 91 (2001), pp. 2039-10l.

51 Though that dysfunction holds for the brain's temporarily crippled executive centers, the brain still makes a hedged bet that can work well. Consider studies of people under extreme stress in settings like firehouses, combat units, and basketball teams. Under dire pressure, the most seasoned leaders did best by relying on habits and expertise formed over years. A fire captain, for instance, could direct his firemen amid the chaotic uncertainty and terror of a blaze by trusting intuitions forged in a long history of similar situations. While old-timers instinctively know what to do in such high-intensity moments, for a novice the best theory can fail. See Fred Fiedler, "The Curious Role of Cognitive Resources in Leadership," in Ronald E. Riggio et al., eds., Multiple Intelligences and Leadership (Mahwah, N.J.: Erlbaum, 2002).

52 On brain correlates of sadness and joy, see Antonio R. Damasio et al., "Subcortical and Cortical Brain Activity During the Feeling of Self-generated

Emotions," Nature Neuroscience 3 (2002), pp. 1049-56.

53 Positive moods, for example, can make people more realistic; when people who are feeling good have an important goal that they want to achieve, they will seek out potentially useful information even when it might be negative and upsetting. See, for example, L. G. Aspinwall, "Rethinking the Role of Positive Affect in Self-regulation," Motivation and Emotion 22 (1998), pp. 1-32. On the other hand, an elevated mood is not necessarily best for every task: being too giddy bodes poorly for detail work like checking a contract. Indeed, negative moods can sometimes make our perceptions more realistic rather than overly rosy. At the right time, it pays to get serious. For a further review, see Neal M. Ashkanasy, "Emotions in Organizations: A Multi-level Perspective," in Neal Ashkanasy et al" eds., Emotions in the Workplace: Research, Theory, and Practice (Westport, Conn.: Quorum BOOks, 2000).

54 On radiologists' diagnoses, see C. A. Estrada et al., "Positive Affect Facilitates Integration of Information and Decreases Anchoring in Reasoning Among Physicians," Organizational Behavior and Human Decision Processes 72 (1997), pp.117-35.

55 Anxiety erodes cognitive efficiency. For example, students with math anxiety have less capacity in their working memory when they tackle a math problem. Their anxiety occupies the attentional space they need for math, impairing their ability to solve math problems or grasp new concepts. See Mark Ashcroft and Elizabeth Kirk, "The Relationship Among Working Memory, Math Anxiety, and Performance," Journal of Experimental Psychology 130, no. 2 (2001), pp.224-27.

56 On cortisol and the inverted U, see Heather C. Abercrombie et al., "Cortisol Variation in Humans Affects Memory for Emotionally Laden and Neutral Information," Behavioral Neuroscience 117 (2003), pp. 505-16.

57 In describing the relationship between mood and performance in terms of the inverted U, I am oversimplifying a bit. Every major emotion has its distinctive influence on how we think. Our moods sway our judgments; when we are in a sour mood, we more readily dislike what we see; in contrast, we are more forgiving or appreciative while we are upbeat. See Neal M. Ashkanasy, "Emotions in Organizations: A Multilevel Perspective," in Neal Ashkanasy et al., eds., Emotions in the Workplace: Research, Theory, and Practice (Westport, Conn.: Quorum Books, 2000). While good moods have great benefits, negative emotions can be useful in specific situations. "Bad" moods can enhance certain kinds of performance, such as attending to detail in a search for errors or making finer distinctions among choices. This mood-task fit has been mapped in more detail in the work of John Mayer at the University of New Hampshire.

For a review of how moods affect performance, see David Caruso et al., The Emotionally Intelligent Manager (San Francisco: Jossey Bass, 2004). Neuroscientists have started to map the specific ways different emotional states might boost various intellectual abilities. In the mild mood range at least, moods can facilitate specific tasks-and on a limited range of specific tasks, negative moods help at times and positive moods sometimes hurt. For instance, anxiety (at least at the levels instilled by watching a clip of a horror film) seems to augment tasks largely processed by the right prefrontal cortex, such as face recognition. Enjoyment (induced by watching a comedy) enhances left-hemisphere tasks such as verbal performance. See Jeremy R. Gray et al., "Integration of Emotion and Cognition in the Lateral Prefrontal Cortex," Proceedings of the National Academy of Sciences 199 (2002), pp. 4115-20.

58 Much the same argument has been made in George and Bettenhausen, "Understanding Prosocial Behavior"; and in Neal N1. Ashkanasy and Barry Tse, "Transformational Leadership as Management of Emotion: A Conceptual Review," in Neal M. Ashkanasy, Charmine E. J. Hartel, and Wilffred J. Zerbe, Emotions in the Workplace: Research, Theory and Practice (Westport, CT: Quorum Books, 2000), 221-235.

The Sweet Spot for Achievement
59 Amy Arnsten, "The Biology of Being Frazzled," Science 280 (1998), pp. 1711-13.

60 Thomas Sy et al., "The Contagious Leader: Impact of the Leader's Mood on the Mood of Group Members, Group Affective Tone, and Group Processes," Journal of Applied Psychology 90 (2005), pp. 295-305.

61 M. T. Dasborough, "Cognitive Asymmetry in Employee Emotional Reactions to Leadership Behaviors," Leadership Quarterly, 17 (2006), pp. 163-178.

62 Neal Ashkanasy et al., "Managing Emotions in a Changing Workplace," in Ashkanasy et al., Emotions in the Workplace.

63 James Harter, Gallup Organization, unpublished report, December 2004.

64 The poll is cited in Amy Zipldn, "The Wisdom of Thoughtfulness," New York Times, May 31, 2000, p. C5.

PERMISSIONS

Managing With Heart
Adapted from Emotional Intelligence, copyright © 1995 by Daniel Goleman. Used by permission of Bantam Books, a division of Random House, Inc.

What Makes a Leader?
Adapted from the Harvard Business Review, January 2004

Leadership that Gets Results
Adapted from the Harvard Business Review, March, 2000

The Group IQ
Adapted from *Emotional Intelligence*, copyright © 1995 by Daniel Goleman. Used by permission of Bantam Books, a division of Random House, Inc.

Primal Leadership
Adapted from *Primal Leadership: Realizing The Power of Emotional Intelligence*, copyright © 2002 by Daniel Goleman. Used by permission of Harvard Business School Press

The Sweet Spot for Achievement
Adapted From *Social Intelligence: The New Science of Human Relationships* by Daniel Goleman, copyright © 2006 by Daniel Goleman. Used by permission of Bantam Books, a division of Random House, Inc.

Appendix
Adapted from *Primal Leadership: Realizing The Power of Emotional Intelligence*, copyright © 2002 by Daniel Goleman. Used by permission of Harvard Business School Press